CW00552094

Smilin' Through and Still Ill

by Billy Cowan

Two Queer plays about Northern Ireland

With a Foreword by John McGrath, Artistic Director of National Theatre Wales

Published by Playdead Press 2014

© Billy Cowan 2014

Billy Cowan has asserted his rights under the Copyright, Design and Patents Act, 1988, to be identified as the author of this work.

A CIP catalogue record for this book is available from the British Library.

ISBN 978-1-910067-27-7

Printed by BPUK

Playdead Press
www.playdeadpress.com

Contents

For Karen, Beth and Kane.

Foreword

Every now and then a theatre script appears that somehow seems more than just vibrant, or well-written, or dramatic – it seems necessary. And when you're artistic director of a theatre and that script's been sent to you, it's your job to respond to that necessity. *Smilin' Through* was one of those scripts. On the surface a highly unlikely combination of post-Good-Friday-agreement Northern Irish politics, a gay coming-out drama, and a nostalgic trip into old Nelson Eddy and Jeanette MacDonald movies, Billy Cowan's script somehow summed up a moment in place and time with an urgency and clarity that was sorely needed.

With a fantastic instinct for theatrical farce, an ear for viciously funny dialogue and a gloriously loveable-awful core character in Peggy Morrow, *Smilin' Through* delights as well as provokes. Cowan can get away with lines like 'One last fuck for Ulster' because the situation in which it is spoken – by the knee-capped ghost of a Loyalist paramilitary as a come-on line to Peggy – is so gloriously absurd. With a vibrantly unsteady boundary between real world and fantasy, the play reminds us that our deeply held convictions, whatever they may be (and the visiting terrorist from the Irish Queer Liberation Army demonstrates that the proponents of liberalism can be as intolerant as any other set of believers), are always only a dance-step away from parodying themselves.

I was delighted that Contact Theatre, where I was Artistic Director at the time, was able to work with the Birmingham Rep, Queerupnorth and the newly formed Truant Company to get the play on stage in 2005. Perhaps in retrospect, this coalition of partners demonstrates one of the questions that faced us in producing the play: what kind of play is it, and who is it for? Whereas Contact reached primarily diverse young people, Birmingham Rep showed the play in its new writing space, and Queerupnorth presented a festival of performance work to predominantly gay and lesbian audiences. That *Smilin' Through* fitted each of these contexts well was to its credit, but also perhaps explains why the play has not been produced more often. It doesn't sit comfortably in the more feel good world of other theatrical coming out dramas, nor match the radical aesthetic of queer performance. It is, in fact, a bit of a queer old mix!

Re-reading it now though, those questions seem much less significant, and, even if the play doesn't quite have the urgency of the moment in the early 2000s when gay and lesbian rights and Northern Irish peace simultaneously shot up the political agenda in the UK, it feels just as resonant now as it did then. I think it now sits confidently in the tradition of the great Irish family dramas – those wild tales of lies and compromise that have been so central to that extraordinary theatrical canon. Amidst all the delightful fantasy and political astuteness, *Smilin' Through* is first and foremost a great love story – the working through of a passionate relationship between a foul-mouthed prejudice-ridden mother and her equally foul-mouthed, lazy-arse gay son. It's a passion built on the boundary between loathing and adoration: '*I couldn't bear it when they put you up to my face. Skinny, slimy, little thing with long legs and arms like a spider. I told the nurse I felt sick so she'd take you away...*' is how Peggy describes her son's arrival in this world to him. And yet, a while later, discovered singing along to Nelson Eddy in his baby basket: '*You looked so beautiful. I lifted you up into my arms and held you tight. From that moment on I grew to love you more than anything ... anyone.*' These aren't Peggy's funniest lines in the play, but they are among her most touching, and they carry us towards the play's conclusion, and the recognition of love, caring, accommodation, that sits with and within the anarchic, vicious world of this wonderfully portrayed family.

There's much else that could be said about *Smilin' Through*. In terms of gay cultural politics it played its own small part in a shift from the radical outsiders of Cowan's Irish Queer Liberation Army to the campaigns for marriage equality of more recent years: when Peggy says of Kyle's boyfriend Donal, '*I'm sure he'll make a lovely son in law,*' it's a joke to both of them, as it was to us all at that time. However, in showing how families – including the seemingly toughest of families – can adjust in their own disruptive, fiery ways to huge shifts in social norms, *Smlin' Through* helped us all imagine a world in which gay sons-in-law might be a new norm.

7

And so it's as a family drama – one which dares to re-imagine family, and even dares to end on an optimistic note about our family futures that *Smilin' Through* ultimately earns its place in the canon. I hope that this publication will bring about many more productions of this still very necessary play.

John McGrath, 2014
Artistic Director, National Theatre of Wales

Smilin' Through was first produced by Contact, the Birmingham Repertory Theatre, Queer Up North and Truant Company. It was first performed at The Birmingham Repertory Theatre on 15th April 2005 with the following cast:

PEGGY MORROW	Gillian Hanna
KYLE MORROW	Marty Rea
DONAL O'SHEA	Terrence Corrigan
WILLY MORROW/	
CARDINAL DAINTY	Walter McMonagle
NELSON EDDY	Alison Harding
REVEREND MCMILLAN/	
R.U.C OFFICER/	
JIM ROBINSON	Sean Kearns

Director	Natalie Wilson
Designer	Emma Donovan
Lighting designer	Emma Chapman
Sound design	Dan Steel

The play received its London premiere at The Drill Hall on 7th November 2007 with the following cast:

PEGGY MORROW	Gillian Hanna
KYLE MORROW	Declan Harvey
DONAL O'SHEA	Russell Simpson
WILLY MORROW/	
CARDINAL DAINTY	Billy Boyle
NELSON EDDY	Wendy Parkin
REVEREND MCMILLAN/	
R.U.C OFFICER/	
JIM ROBINSON	Colm Gormley

Director	Natalie Wilson
Designer	Neil Irish
Lighting designer	Nao Nagai
Sound design	David Willis

The play won the 2003 Writing Out Award for Best New Gay Play organised by The Finborough Theatre, London. It was nominated for Best New Play 2005 by the Manchester Evening News Theatre Awards.

Characters

Peggy Morrow – A hardened Presbyterian housewife in her fifties

Willy Morrow – Peggy's long-suffering husband

Kyle Morrow – Their twenty-two year old son

Donal O'Shea – Kyle's boyfriend

An R.U.C. Officer

A member of a protestant paramilitary organisation

Fantasy characters

Nelson Eddy – A dyke parading as the dead Hollywood movie star

Reverend McMillan – A fire and brimstone Presbyterian Minister

Cardinal Dainty – A Catholic Bishop

Jim Robinson – A dead terrorist

A member of the Irish Queer Liberation Army

The play is set in an East Belfast house just as the Good Friday Agreement is about to be signed. We can see the living room and Kyle's bedroom. The actor playing Willy can double up as the Cardinal and the actor playing Reverend McMillan can also play the RUC Officer, the protestant paramilitary member and Jim Robinson.

All rights to perform the songs must be obtained from the relevant copyright sources.

One

Peggy stands alone singing Smilin' Through by Arthur A. Penn. She is dressed like a movie star. She looks younger than her years and radiates with warmth and kindness.

Two

Morning. Living room. The radio is on and the newscaster talks about the signing of the Good Friday Agreement. Willy sits reading The Sun. He wears a postman's uniform. We can also see Kyle lying asleep in his bed. Peggy enters from the kitchen and turns the radio off.

PEGGY: Fuckin' Peace Agreement!

She looks older than the first scene and the warm personality has gone. She starts to dust the furniture and then moves to Kyle's bedroom door where she bangs on it with her fist, laughing. Kyle jolts and places his head under his pillow. Peggy bangs on the door again and again until Kyle is enraged.

KYLE: Piss off!

PEGGY: Get up you lazy shite.

KYLE: I'll get up when I feel like it.

PEGGY: It's one o'clock. Do you want to lie in bed all day?

KYLE: SHUT UP!

WILY: Boy, you're an evil woman Peggy.

PEGGY: And you're a soft shite.

Peggy goes to an old stereo music centre and puts on a Jeanette MacDonald and Nelson Eddy record. She turns it up loud.

WILY: For goodness sake!

Kyle jumps off the bed and flings the bedroom door open.

KYLE: Turn that off now or I'll smash your face in!

Peggy laughs and Kyle slams the door shut. She turns the music up louder, then sits down on the settee and lights up a cigarette. Kyle turns his CD player on and The Prodigy's 'Firestarter' comes belting out. He pulls on a pair of tracksuit bottoms. Peggy runs to the bedroom door.

PEGGY: Turn that crap off!

Kyle turns it up louder.

(*To Willy*) Are you just going to sit there?

WILY: Hey son, turn that music down!

Willy marches over to the stereo and turns Jeanette MacDonald and Nelson Eddy off.

PEGGY: (*To Willy*) Hey you!

Kyle turns his music off and comes out of his room.

PEGGY: Oh, the dead arose and appeared to many.

KYLE: Do you have to be such an aggravating bitch?

PEGGY: Do you have to be such a lazy bastard?

KYLE: Give your mouth a rest, will you?

He exits into the kitchen.

PEGGY: And don't be making a mess in there.

WILY: Do you two never shut up?

PEGGY: Ah sit there Ghandi and read your bloody newspaper.

WILY: It's a sad state of affairs, Peggy, when a man can't read his paper in peace.

PEGGY: You're lucky that's all you've got to worry about. If you were one of the Robinsons you'd have a lot more on your plate than a pair of tits in the bloody newspaper.

WILY: What have they got to worry about?

PEGGY: Jim Robinson. He's dead. The bastards finally got him.

Willy is unconcerned.

PEGGY: Don't you care one of your neighbours has been killed?

WILY: He was asking for it. Live by the sword, die by the sword.

14

PEGGY: At least he was doing something for his fuckin' country. Not sitting on his arse like the rest of yous.

WILY: He was lining his own pockets.

PEGGY: He was a man. More than I can say for you.

WILY: He was a murderer.

PEGGY: He was protecting his heritage.

WILY: Don't talk nonsense woman.

PEGGY: If I'd a gun, I'd be doing the same thing.

WILY: You're a bloody nutcase.

PEGGY: Thirty-five years with you has made me this way.

WILY: No one asked you to stay.

PEGGY: If I'd had somewhere else to go I would have went years ago.

WILY: Well what's stopping you now?

PEGGY: Oh no, Sonny Jim. This is my house. If anyone goes it'll be you. I'm the one who's decorated every one of these fuckin' walls, bought every piece of furniture. You haven't even put a bloody nail in the wall,

15

for Christ's sake. No, this is my house. If anyone goes it'll be you. Remember that.

Willy loses the rag.

WILY: I'm off to work.

PEGGY: Yeah, you do that. And while you're at it, why don't you stick yourself in one of those sacks and post yourself as far away from here as possible.

WILY: I might just do that. At least I'd get some peace.

PEGGY: Don't think I'd give a damn. I'm long past caring about you.

WILY: So you keep saying.

PEGGY: And so I'll keep on saying.

Willy exits. Kyle enters from the kitchen with his breakfast on a tray.

KYLE: What are you looking at?

PEGGY: Right now, my two eyes are full of shit.

KYLE: And so's your mouth.

PEGGY: What time did you crawl home at this morning?

KYLE: What's it to you?

16

PEGGY:	I'm your mother.
KYLE:	And I'm twenty-two.
PEGGY:	You're still living under my roof.
KYLE:	It doesn't give you the right to know my every move.
PEGGY:	I suppose you were out with that fenian friend of yours?
KYLE:	Why ask when you know you won't get an answer?
PEGGY:	I wonder why?
KYLE:	Coz it's none of your business.
PEGGY:	Is that right?
KYLE:	Yeah.
PEGGY:	Maybe you just don't want me finding out.
KYLE:	Finding out what?
PEGGY:	You tell me.
KYLE:	There's nothing to tell.
PEGGY:	That's not what I heard.
KYLE:	What are you talking about?

17

PEGGY: I don't take kindly to being stopped in the street by someone I barely know and being told something about my own bloody son.

KYLE: Well then, tell them to mind their own fucking business.

PEGGY: Don't worry son, they didn't get the better of me.

KYLE: Then what's your problem?

PEGGY: It'id be nice to hear it from my own son first.

KYLE: Hear what?

PEGGY: Oh no, son. If you've got something to tell me then I want you to say it.

KYLE: Look Ma, shut up. There's nothing to hear. I don't know why you keep doing this.

PEGGY: To keep you on your toes.

KYLE: Okay. I'm on my toes. I'm fuckin' dancing. Now give it a rest. Let me eat my breakfast in peace.

PEGGY: Peace, peace, peace. It's all everyone thinks about at the moment.

KYLE: Change the record. It's too early in the morning to be listening to McMillan's number one fan.

PEGGY: That's the kind of attitude that has got us where we are today.

KYLE: I don't want to get into this.

PEGGY: When will you? When it's too late? Sure, it's too late already. We're living under the green, white and gold now for Christ's sake.

KYLE: You're boring me!

PEGGY: We'll see how bored you are when you can't get a job because all those fenian fuckers have taken over.

KYLE: Don't talk shite.

PEGGY: Those English bastards have sold us down the river Lagan and into the South. Never trust an Englishman.

Kyle repeats 'Never trust an Englishman' at the same time as Peggy – he's heard it all before.

KYLE: Never trust an Englishman. Yabber, yabber, yabber. If you feel that way why do you want to be British?

PEGGY: I don't want to be British. I just don't want to be Irish more.

KYLE: What do you want to be then – Turkish?

PEGGY: I want to be what I am – a Northern Irish Protestant.

KYLE:	Sure you're no Protestant. When was the last time you set foot in a church?
PEGGY:	I am a Protestant politically, not religiously.
KYLE:	Sitting on your fat arse on the edge of the settee and calling everyone a fenian bastard does not make you political.
PEGGY:	I know who the enemy is, that's all that matters.
KYLE:	The Holy Roman Church.
PEGGY:	Yes, and don't forget it.
KYLE:	(*Laughing*) You're a bloody dinosaur, woman. No one gives a shit about the church anymore – not even the Catholics. The Holy Roman Church has as much influence as a copper during the marching season.
PEGGY:	That's what it wants us to think, but it still controls everything.
KYLE:	I doubt anything could control you.
PEGGY:	Just look at Africa. All those black heathens were once free and happy, running about the plains naked and killing animals. And now look at them – running about with rosary beads, chanting Hail

	Mary's and asking for forgiveness. What chance have we got?
KYLE:	And what about the Free Presbyterians? They've gone to Africa as well, you know. McMillan goes there all the time.
PEGGY:	You leave him out of this. He's a true man of God.
KYLE:	He's no different from the Catholics. They're all the fuckin' same.
PEGGY:	You don't get McMillan sitting at a table talking to murderers, do you?
KYLE:	Not yet, but he'll have to do it sooner or later.
PEGGY:	McMillan will never do that!
KYLE:	Look I'm not getting into this. We've got peace for a while and that counts for something.
PEGGY:	We do not have peace! We will never have peace. Too many people have been hurt, and forgiveness doesn't come easy. And nor should it.
KYLE:	Can't you fucking find something else to think about?

PEGGY: Oh, I think about a lot of things, son. Don't
                 you worry about that.

KYLE: You can sit here and think about what the
                 fuck you like. I've had enough.

He goes to his bedroom, slamming the door.

PEGGY: Yeah, run to your bedroom. Can't take it,
                 can you? You're a weakling, like your Da.

She lights a cigarette.

Three

Late afternoon. Kyle is reading. There's a knock at the door. Kyle answers it.

DONAL: Hi ya.

KYLE: Am I glad to see you!

He pulls Donal into the house. They kiss.

DONAL: I take it she's gone then?

KYLE: Yeah, she's in the pub. We've got the house to ourselves.

He leads Donal to the settee.

DONAL: Are you sure she won't be back?

KYLE: Don't worry, they usually have to throw her out.

They kiss again. Kyle tries to take Donal's trousers down. Donal resists.

KYLE: What's the matter?

DONAL: I don't feel comfortable ...

KYLE: ...Fuck sake.

DONAL: ...doing it here... in your Ma's house.

KYLE: It's my house as well, you know.

DONAL: It just doesn't feel right.

KYLE:	Yous Catholics are all the same.
DONAL:	It's got nothing to do with being a Catholic.
KYLE:	Oh yeah?
DONAL:	I just don't think it's fair.
KYLE:	You see, guilt. Catholic guilt.
DONAL:	Look don't start.
KYLE:	Once a Catholic always a Catholic.
DONAL:	That's not true, Kyle. You know I don't believe in any of that nonsense.
KYLE:	Why do you still go to Mass then?
DONAL:	I'm not getting into this.
KYLE:	You do it to please your Ma. And why do you feel the need to please your Ma? (*Donal doesn't reply.*) Guilt.
DONAL:	It's not guilt, it's compassion.
KYLE:	Same thing in my book.
DONAL:	I do it to make her happy. What's wrong with that?
KYLE:	You're a hypocrite, that's what's wrong with it.

DONAL:	Sometimes you have to put other people's feelings first.
KYLE:	I'd never compromise my principles for anyone else.
DONAL:	Even for me?
KYLE:	Well that depends on what you've got to offer.

Kyle tries to undo his trousers again.

DONAL:	Don't!
KYLE:	The trouble with you is - you're still repressed.
DONAL:	No, I'm not.
KYLE:	Donal, you don't even allow yourself to swear.
DONAL:	Bad language shows a lack of vocabulary.
KYLE:	And you never get angry.
DONAL:	That's because it doesn't solve anything.
KYLE:	If someone was to come up to you and kick you in the balls for no good reason, you'd say sorry.
DONAL:	Don't be ridiculous.

KYLE:	Admit it? You're repressed in every single way.
DONAL:	And what about you? You haven't even come out to your Ma yet.
KYLE:	Yeah, well she's going to know soon enough.
DONAL:	I've heard that before.
KYLE:	I mean it. I'm telling her, tonight.
DONAL:	What's brought this on?
KYLE:	There's been talk on the street. And I'm sick of all her bloody innuendoes. She's driving me fuckin' mad.
DONAL:	Are you sure it's what you want to do?
KYLE:	Too right I'm sure. It's time to stand up and be counted.
DONAL:	I'm glad.

Donal smiles and kisses Kyle tenderly on the lips.

DONAL:	There's something I want to ask you. (*Pause*) I've been looking at this really nice flat in the Holy Lands. And... I was just wondering whether you'd... well like to... maybe move in with me. (*Kyle is shocked.*) It just seems that now might be a good time.

KYLE: Fuck sake, Donal. That's a bit sudden.

DONAL: I thought we could give it a go. I mean, it doesn't have to be forever or anything... but... Don't you want to live with me?

Kyle hesitates. A key is heard being put in the door.

KYLE: Shit, that's her.

DONAL: What'll I do?

KYLE: Just... just sit down over there.

Kyle pushes him over to the armchair. He reaches it just as Peggy comes through the door. She's drunk.

KYLE: Here comes the pisshead.

PEGGY: I am not pissed, you cheeky little bast... (*She sees Donal*) rascal.

Kyle laughs.

KYLE: This is Donal, Ma. You've met him before.

PEGGY: I can see that. (*To Donal*) He thinks I'm bloody stupid.

Peggy falls onto the settee.

PEGGY: So Donal. How are things with you?

DONAL: Fine, Mrs Morrow.

PEGGY: Still out of work?

27

DONAL:	Well actually, I'm at…
KYLE:	…He's at University.
PEGGY:	Ach never mind. There's a lot in the same boat.
DONAL:	Yes.
PEGGY:	Things'll get worse when we become one. Just wait and see. There'll be no work for anyone, especially us Protestants. We'll have to…
KYLE:	…Yes, Ma. I'm sure Donal doesn't want to sit here and listen to you going on about the plight of us poor Protestants.
DONAL:	That's okay. You can talk about whatever you like, Mrs Morrow.
PEGGY:	Well thank you, Donal. At least someone shows me a bit of respect in my own home. He never shows me any.
KYLE:	You never deserve it.
PEGGY:	Do you hear that, Donal? Do you speak to your Ma like that?
DONAL:	No.
PEGGY:	(*To Kyle*) You see.
KYLE:	That's because he's afraid of her.

PEGGY: Mothers are meant to be feared!

KYLE: And here's me thinking they wanted to be loved.

PEGGY: Mothers want respect more than love. We want obedience from our weans – not cheek.

KYLE: You think children should be slaves, is that it?

PEGGY: They should be there to make life easier for their mothers, not more difficult.

KYLE: Even if the mother is a mad, evil, aul bitch?

PEGGY: Yes! Because her family's probably made her that way.

KYLE: You weren't made that way – you were born that way.

PEGGY: At least I wasn't born a... (queer)

KYLE: A what?

Pause.

PEGGY: A cheeky little bastard.

KYLE: I think it's time we got going, Donal. Before she starts on one.

PEGGY: Nonsense. Have a cup of tea before you go.

DONAL: I was meant to be somewhere by…

PEGGY: …It'll only take a minute to have a wee cup of tea.

KYLE: He doesn't want a cup of tea.

PEGGY: Of course he does! And so do I. You'll have a wee cup of tea with me, won't you Donal?

DONAL: Well… okay.

PEGGY: Great. Kyle, go and make the tea and bring in some of those nice buns I got yesterday down at The Bride's Parlour.

KYLE: Why can't you make it?

PEGGY: Because I can't get up outta this seat. (*To Donal*) I've had a wee too much to drink.

KYLE: You don't say.

PEGGY: Are you going to make the tea or not?

KYLE: I'm going, I'm going.

He exits.

PEGGY: And don't make a mess.

KYLE: (*From kitchen*) Drop dead.

Peggy lights a cigarette and moves very close to Donal.

PEGGY:	So. Donal. How's things? Been anywhere interesting? Done anything you shouldn't have?
DONAL:	Um... no.
PEGGY:	Did you go out with Kyle last night?
DONAL:	Yes.
PEGGY:	Where did you go?
DONAL:	Oh... just out in town.
PEGGY:	Did you go dancing?
DONAL:	No. I'm not really into dancing.
PEGGY:	I used to love it when I was your age. Willy and I used to go to the Queen's Hall every Saturday. It was brilliant. If you ask me, yous youngsters don't know how to enjoy yourselves. Or maybe you just get your kicks in different ways. How do you get your kicks, Donal?

Donal is petrified. Peggy is enjoying herself.

DONAL:	Um... um... the cinema, I suppose.
PEGGY:	The back row, I bet.
DONAL:	Oh no, not at all.
PEGGY:	What? A good looking boy like you. Now if it was my Kyle, I could understand it. I

31

mean, he's not the prettiest sash in the parade. Is he, Donal?

Donal doesn't know how to respond. Peggy laughs.

He used to be such a good boy, you know. Well behaved. Do anything for me. When he was younger he would sit in and keep me company. We'd sit with a bag of raspberry ruffles and watch all the old movies together. He was a great son... then. God only knows what happened, for now he's a little bastard who goes out of his way to annoy me.

Kyle re-enters with tea things.

KYLE: What are you mouthing about now?

PEGGY: I was just telling Donal how you used to be the perfect son who'd do anything for his mother.

KYLE: That's before I realised you were a manipulating, aul bitch.

PEGGY: Oh is that right?

KYLE: And a control freak who likes to get her own way even when she knows she's in the wrong.

PEGGY: I'm never in the wrong.

KYLE:	Oh yes, and what about our Anne?
PEGGY:	I'm warning you, son. Just shut your mouth.
KYLE:	Well just remember, mommie dearest, that's why I changed.
PEGGY:	You changed because of the company you started to keep.
KYLE:	Like who?

Peggy glances at Donal.

PEGGY:	Like ones... from the other side.
KYLE:	And that's another thing that made me see the truth about you... your bigotry!
PEGGY:	I am not a bigot. I take people for what they are and what they stand for. If they stand for murder then of course I'm against them.
KYLE:	Even the loyalist paramilitaries?
PEGGY:	Yes.
KYLE:	You're a lying bitch. You condone everything they do.
PEGGY:	I do not.
KYLE:	Yes you do. You just don't want to say so in front of Donal.

33

PEGGY: If I want to say something in my own home, I'll say it, no matter who's here.

KYLE: Go on then, admit it. Tell Donal that you condone what they do.

PEGGY: Don't listen to him, Donal. He's just trying to rile me. I do not condone what they do... unless, of course, it's in retaliation.

KYLE: (*Laughing*) You see.

PEGGY: What? Are you saying to me that if someone killed me or your Da, you wouldn't want to get revenge?

KYLE: I'd thank them.

PEGGY: Oh, that's nice. Isn't it Donal? Is it any wonder we're losing the battle.

KYLE: The only battle you're losing is with the vodka.

PEGGY: I can control my drinking, son. It's a pity you can't control your mouth.

KYLE: When I start spouting as much shit as you then I'll control it.

PEGGY: Oh, he thinks he's so clever, Donal. How do you put up with it?

Peggy's question hints at a more than platonic relationship between Kyle and Donal. Kyle panics.

KYLE:	It's time you caught your bus, Donal. Come on, before she starts again.
PEGGY:	But you haven't finished your buns yet.
KYLE:	I've had more than I can stomach, thank you.
PEGGY:	Piss off then.
KYLE:	Get stuffed.
PEGGY:	Bastard
KYLE:	Whore.

Kyle and Donal leave.

Four

Evening. Peggy lies on the settee, sleeping. It starts to snow and Nelson Eddy appears. She goes over to Peggy and starts to sing to her – Indian Love Call by Harbach & Hammerstein II. Willy enters and Nelson disappears. He sits down and pulls out The Sun, reading the back pages. Peggy wakes. Willy ignores her. She grabs one of the buns and throws it at his paper.

PEGGY: Your son was here with his wee friend when I got back.

WILY: What friend?

PEGGY: Fenian Donal from Ardglass.

WILY: Didn't know he had a friend called Donal.

PEGGY: That's hardly surprising.

WILY: Don't start, Peggy.

PEGGY: Well if you took an interest in your son, I wouldn't need to. All you care about is your bloody golf or how much overtime you can get. Maybe if you'd shown some interest in your son he wouldn't have turned out queer.

WILY: What are you talking about?

PEGGY: Your son is a queer.

WILY: Don't talk nonsense.

PEGGY: Open your eyes for God's sake. Why do you think he never brings any girls home – it's because he's gay, queer whatever you call them. Him and that Donal one.

WILY: Can't two boys be friends without you bringing something else into it?

PEGGY: He's queer! Look at the way he acts and speaks, and you should see how he and that Donal one get on. Cheeky little glances to each other; little courting smiles. It's disgusting.

WILY: You're the one who's disgusting.

PEGGY: I will not tell you again – your son is a shite thumper!

WILY: Well, what if he is? We can't all be the same. Live and let live, Peggy.

PEGGY: If people round here find out, he won't be able to live. Is that what you want?

WILY: It's his life. He has to make his own choices. Let him do what he wants.

PEGGY: While he's under this roof he'll do as I say.

WILY: You can't stop him being queer if that's the way he is.

37

PEGGY: No? Well then, he can pack his bags and go.

WILY: Not again, Peggy. I thought you'd have learned by now.

PEGGY: No son of mine is queer.

WILY: If he is you've made him that way. You're the one who smothered him, spoilt him rotten.

PEGGY: And why was that, eh? Eh? Because I wasn't getting any fuckin' love from you, that's why. If you'd been a real husband none of this would have happened.

WILY: There's always someone else to blame. Isn't there, Peggy?

PEGGY: I want him out of the house.

WILY: You don't even know for sure if he is…

PEGGY: He is!

WILY: Has he told you?

PEGGY: He doesn't need to. I'm his mother.

WILY: It's probably all in your filthy mind.

PEGGY: We'll see. We'll see.

WILY: Don't you be starting any trouble tonight. Do you hear? Just let it go.

PEGGY: Anything for a quiet life. Well, not this time. I'm going to get it out of him.

WILY: Please yourself Peggy, but just remember what happened to our Anne.

PEGGY: Don't you dare... (bring that up.)

WILY: You pushed her too far and now you're going to do the same with him. Is that what you want? To lose him as well.

PEGGY: Let him go! He'll be sorry, believe me.

Kyle enters.

KYLE: You still here. I thought you'd have passed out by now.

PEGGY: Oh I'm awake, son. Wide awake.

KYLE: Good for fucking you.

WILY: The film's on in half an hour.

Willy goes to turn the TV on.

PEGGY: The TV stays off! If you want to watch the film you can go upstairs.

Willy walks to the door.

WILY: (*To Peggy*) Remember what I said.

Willy exits.

KYLE: What was that about?

PEGGY: Nothing.

KYLE: I see. Like that, is it?

PEGGY: Did Donal catch his bus okay?

KYLE: Yes. Thanks for asking.

PEGGY: He's a strange boy, isn't he?

KYLE: Not as strange as you.

PEGGY: He looks kind of… funny. Queer looking.

KYLE: Bollocks.

PEGGY: He's a nervous creature.

KYLE: Only when he's around you.

PEGGY: No, it's something else.

KYLE: Yeah, like what?

PEGGY: I don't know. It's as if he's hiding something.

KYLE: Well what do you think it is, Inspector Morse?

PEGGY: He's your friend. You tell me.

KYLE: Maybe he's a terrorist.

PEGGY: Maybe.

KYLE: Look, what are you playing at?

PEGGY: It's not me who's playing games.

KYLE: So I'm playing games, am I?

PEGGY: Are you?

KYLE: Look Ma, if you really want me to stop playing games I will. But you won't like it.

PEGGY: I can take it.

KYLE: Can you?

PEGGY: I can take anything.

KYLE: I wouldn't be too sure about that.

PEGGY: Try me.

Pause.

KYLE: Okay, no more games. I, Kyle Morrow, am gay. I'm bent, queer. A fairy, whatever you want to call it.

PEGGY: I want you out of the house.

KYLE: I don't think you do.

PEGGY: Get out.

KYLE: Oh, that's great. Isn't it? No discussion, just a 'Get out.' It's nice to know you care mother.

PEGGY: How can I care when you show no regard for me or how I feel?

41

KYLE: It's not a choice, you know.

PEGGY: It's a choice when you lie down with another man. No one puts a gun to your head.

KYLE: What do you expect me to do? Become a monk or something.

PEGGY: I don't care what you do as long as it's not in my house.

KYLE: Oh you approve if it's not under your nose, is that it?

PEGGY: I'll never approve of what you do. It's disgusting. Now I want you out of the house.

KYLE: Well, if that's what you want mother then that's what you'll get.

He stomps towards the bedroom door, but then hesitates. He turns back.

No. Why should I? That's too easy for you, isn't it? Well, I'm not going anywhere. I have as much right to stay here as you. This is my house as well, you know. I'm staying.

Peggy flies off the settee.

PEGGY: It is my house!

KYLE: I don't care. I'm staying.

PEGGY: Get out!

KYLE: If you want me out you'll have to physically throw me out.

PEGGY: Don't think I wouldn't, son. I'm not past it yet. Now pack your things, I want you outta here by tomorrow.

KYLE: I'm going nowhere.

PEGGY: I want you outta this house!

KYLE: I'm going nowhere!

PEGGY: Don't raise your voice to me! Now get out.

KYLE: No.

PEGGY: Get out!

KYLE: No.

PEGGY: You'll do as I say, you dirty fuckin pervert!

Kyle goes to hit her.

PEGGY: Go on! Go on. Try it. I dare you. Go on!

Kyle thinks about it and then slaps her across the face. He runs to his bedroom and slams the door shut. He throws himself onto the bed.

Five

Later. Peggy lies sleeping on the settee. Nelson Eddy enters singing the beginning of Indian Love Call. Peggy wakes.

PEGGY: Who are you? And what the fuck are you doing in my house?

NELSON: I was hoping you could tell me, Peggy.

PEGGY: How do you know my name?

NELSON: Maybe we've met before.

PEGGY: We don't get many Mounties around these parts. I'd remember.

NELSON: Memories are easily buried.

PEGGY: I never forget a face.

NELSON: Then come closer and have another look.

PEGGY: Piss off!

NELSON: I like a girl with a fiery temperament.

PEGGY: Get out of my house!

NELSON: Are you trying to seduce me?

PEGGY: Look, what do you want?

NELSON: Music and lights, fun and laughter.

PEGGY: Well you've come to the wrong house.

NELSON: Oh, Peggy. You take the heart out of me.
                Now be a good girl and let's play a game.

Nelson produces a dress.

PEGGY: Here, I think I know you. What's your
                name?

NELSON: Nelson Eddy, who else?

PEGGY: You're not Nelson Eddy. He was more
                handsome than you. More manly. No, I
                know who you are... I just can't put my
                finger on it yet.

NELSON: Here put these on. We're gonna play a
                game.

PEGGY: You must think I'm soft in the head.

NELSON: Don't you trust me?

PEGGY: I've learnt to trust no-one.

NELSON: It's time you started then. Now be a good
                sport and put the dress on.

PEGGY: Like hell!

NELSON: You're going to be my Jeanette
                MacDonald.

PEGGY: I'm not Jeanette MacDonald and you're
                certainly not Nelson Eddy.

NELSON: Just use your imagination.

45

PEGGY: I'll stick to reality, if that's okay with you?

NELSON: You're a stubborn mare, aren't you?

PEGGY: It's one of my better qualities.

NELSON: Maybe you need reigned in.

PEGGY: There's no-one man enough.

NELSON: Is that a challenge?

Peggy shrugs her shoulders.

I'm going to enjoy this assignment. Now put the dress on.

PEGGY: No.

NELSON: What is it you're afraid of, Peggy? Afraid of letting go, maybe? Of losing control?

Peggy is taken aback.

PEGGY: I'm afraid of nothing, especially an apparition in a bloody Mounties uniform.

NELSON: When was the last time you had some fun? The last time you felt like a million dollars, Peggy? Can you remember?

PEGGY: A long time ago.

NELSON: Don't you think you deserve some fun then? (*Pause.*) I think you do. (*Pause*) Come on, try it. You might even like it.

She holds out the dress. Peggy hesitates, but then suddenly grabs it.

PEGGY: Give me the bloody things, but I'm warning you. If anything untoward happens - I'll have you.

Nelson laughs as Peggy puts the dress and wig on.

NELSON: That's a girl.

A perceivable change comes over Peggy when the dress is on. Nelson takes her in her arms and they sing Indian Love Call.

PEGGY: I feel like a star.

NELSON: You're the moon and the stars, Peggy.

PEGGY: I'm too old to fall for lines like that, but don't stop.

NELSON: The universe resides in your heart. A world is born every time you breathe. When you close your eyes angels sleep. Your hair / is the...

PEGGY: Ok, stop. My imagination will only stretch so far.

NELSON: Your imagination knows no limits.

47

PEGGY:	You talk a load of shit, but I do like you.
NELSON:	I'm glad. It'll make my job easier.
PEGGY:	And what's that?
NELSON:	You tell me.
PEGGY:	Oh God! Can't you just give me a straight answer for once?
NELSON:	You have the answers already.
PEGGY:	You're my guardian angel, is that it?
NELSON:	I am what you want me to be.
PEGGY:	Christ, you're annoying!
NELSON:	It's one of my better qualities.
PEGGY:	That's it. I want you to go.
NELSON:	Nonsense.
PEGGY:	I do. Now piss off.
NELSON:	Okay, but she comes with me. Now give the dress back.
PEGGY:	No way!
NELSON:	I'm taking her back.

Nelson attempts to take the wig from her.

PEGGY:	Clear off! She's mine.

NELSON:	Give her back.
PEGGY:	No. I'm not ready.
NELSON:	I'll have to use force.
PEGGY:	I'm a strong woman.
NELSON:	You used to be.
PEGGY:	I still am. Try me.
NELSON:	If that's what you want.

Nelson chases Peggy around the settee. Peggy is screaming. She quickly runs out of breath. Nelson gets her in an arm-lock.

NELSON:	Do you surrender?
PEGGY:	Never. This is my house. No surrender!

Nelson rips the dress off.

NELSON:	A house full of hate and anger is not worth the bricks it was built with.
PEGGY:	It's the only one I've got and nobody is going to take it away from me.
NELSON:	Nobody wants to, but you have to learn how to share it and I will show you the way.
PEGGY:	I don't need help from outsiders.
NELSON:	You need help from wherever you can get it, Peggy. You can't be trusted to sort it out by yourself.

49

PEGGY: Piss off!

NELSON: You're weak.

PEGGY: Get out! Go on, fuck off!

NELSON: Alright, Peggy. You're the boss.

Nelson goes to leave.

PEGGY: And don't bother coming back. I never asked you to come in the first place.

NELSON: Don't fret. I won't desert you in your hour of need.

PEGGY: I don't care if you never come back.

NELSON: Splendid!

Nelson exits.

Six

Late morning. Peggy sits in the corner of the settee, smoking a cigarette. Kyle sits on his bed flicking through a magazine.

PEGGY:	It's my fuckin' house!
KYLE:	So you keep fuckin' saying!
PEGGY:	You can't stay barricaded in there forever.
KYLE:	I'll stay for as long as it takes.
PEGGY:	You'll starve.
KYLE:	I'm on HUNGER STRIKE!
PEGGY:	Martyrdom's only for Catholics, didn't you know that?
KYLE:	Maybe I'll turn.
PEGGY:	What have you got to lose – you're already a sodomite.
KYLE:	And you're the mother of one.

Peggy flies off the settee and runs to the bedroom. Kyle jumps off his bed.

PEGGY:	Look, I've had enough of this.
KYLE:	How do you think I feel? I'm the one who's starving.
PEGGY:	Well then, get out.

51

KYLE: Not until you admit that you're in the wrong.

PEGGY: You'll be waiting a quare long time before that happens.

KYLE: That's okay. I'm not going anywhere.

PEGGY: Look, if you don't get out now I'll... I'll... get the peelers to throw you out.

KYLE: (*Laughing*) They'd laugh in your face, you stupid, aul bitch.

PEGGY: We'll soon see, son.

She throws on a coat and exits. Kyle hunts around his bedroom for food. From under his bed he pulls out the leftovers of an old pizza. It's as hard as rock, but he tries to crunch through it. Willy enters wearing his postman's uniform.

KYLE: Da, is that you?

Willy jumps out of his skin.

WILY: Jesus!

WILY: You scared the living daylights out of me. I thought no-one was in.

KYLE: You couldn't fetch us a cup of tea, could you?

WILY: What's going on? Why aren't you coming out?

KYLE:	Hasn't she told you what's happened?
WILY:	She never tells me anything.
KYLE:	We've had a… disagreement.
WILY:	Well there's nothing new there son.
KYLE:	It's serious this time. I've barricaded myself in.
WILY:	Oh dear God.
KYLE:	She hasn't told you anything? (*Pause.*) Da?
WILY:	She told me she thinks you're a…
KYLE:	A what?
WILY:	Nothing. Nothing, son.
KYLE:	That I'm queer?
WILY:	I'll get you that tea son.
KYLE:	She wants me out, Da. But I'm not going. I want her to realise she's in the wrong. I want her to admit that she still cares… no matter what I am.
WILY:	Maybe you should just leave, son. Give her a bit of time to get used to it.
KYLE:	If I leave I won't be back.

WILY:	But you can't stay cooped up in there. You know how stubborn she is.
KYLE:	So am I.
WILY:	I'm not sure this is the right way to go about it. You know how she likes a good fight.
KYLE:	We all have to compromise at some point.
WILY:	Your mother's a Presbyterian.
KYLE:	It's time she learned.
WILY:	I admire your courage, son.
KYLE:	You could help, Da. Have a word with her.
WILY:	She never listens to me.
KYLE:	You could try.
WILY:	I'll only get accused of being soft.
KYLE:	Well stand up to her. (*Pause.*) Anne might still be alive today if you'd stood up to her.
Silence.	
WILY:	Don't you think I tried, son?
KYLE:	You could have tried harder.

WILY:	Nothing I said made a difference. Your mother hated that Robinson boy. There was no way she was going to budge.
KYLE:	Anne should have told her to fuck off and married him anyway.
WILY:	She worshipped your mother. She didn't want to upset her.
KYLE:	Well, I'm not as soft.
WILY:	No. You're cut from the same cloth as your Ma.
KYLE:	Yeah, and it's time I stood up to her.

Pause.

WILY:	Maybe you're right.
KYLE:	Will you have a word with her then?
WILY:	Okay, I'll try. But I don't think it will make a difference. Where is she anyway?
KYLE:	She's getting the police.
WILY:	Oh dear God.
KYLE:	You couldn't get me something to eat, Da, before she comes back?
WILY:	As long as you don't tell her.

Willy goes into the kitchen. Peggy enters with a policeman.

55

OFFICER:	I'm not sure whether I can interfere in this, Mrs Morrow. It sounds like a domestic situation.
PEGGY:	Look Officer, as far as I'm concerned there's a trespasser in my house who refuses to get out. Now surely you can have him arrested or something?
OFFICER:	But didn't you say he was your son?
PEGGY:	He's no son of mine.
OFFICER:	(*Checking his notebook*) But I'm sure you said he was.
PEGGY:	He may have sprouted from my womb, but that was a long time ago. He's a stranger to me now.
OFFICER:	He's still your son as far as biology and the law is concerned.
PEGGY:	As far as I'm concerned he's a squatter.
OFFICER:	A squatter?
PEGGY:	Yes, a squatter. Now, are you going to do something about it or not?
OFFICER:	I suppose I can try, but I can't guarantee anything.
PEGGY:	I learnt along time ago not to rely on the police.

OFFICER:	Now, now, Mrs Morrow.
PEGGY:	So don't worry about smashing any illusions I have about your usefulness.
OFFICER:	We do our best.
PEGGY:	Just get over there and tell him to get out.

She pushes him over to the bedroom door.

OFFICER:	Hallo … you in there. Can you hear me?
KYLE:	Of course I can. You're only a few inches away, you know.
PEGGY:	Less of your cheek. (*To Officer*) You see what I have to put up with, Officer.
OFFICER:	This is Officer Kildare. Your mother tells me that you refuse to leave her house.
KYLE:	It's my house as well.
OFFICER:	It is your mother's house.
KYLE:	I pay rent.
OFFICER:	(*To Peggy*) Does he?
PEGGY:	Not bloody much.
OFFICER:	Oh I see. This puts a different light on things. Tenants have certain rights, Mrs Morrow.

57

PEGGY:	He's not a tenant. There's no written agreement between us. So he hasn't a leg to stand on.
OFFICER:	(*Shouting to Kyle*) Your mother tells me that…
KYLE:	There's no need to shout.
OFFICER:	…that there is no tenancy agreement. In the eyes of the law this means she can throw you out whenever she wants.
KYLE:	So much for British justice.
OFFICER:	You'll leave then?
KYLE:	No way!
OFFICER:	This is a serious offence. You're obstructing the Law.
KYLE:	Fuck the law. It's never been on my side anyway.
OFFICER:	The Law does not take sides.
PEGGY:	Except when it comes to the marching season.
OFFICER:	What was that Mrs Morrow?
PEGGY:	Nothing, nothing Officer.
OFFICER:	So you refuse to come out?

KYLE: Got it in one.

Willy enters with a tray, carrying a plate of beans and toast.

PEGGY: I hope that's not for who I think it's for.

WILY: Get out of my way, Peggy.

PEGGY: Make me.

WILY: He has to eat.

PEGGY: He's on hunger strike.

OFFICER: Oh dear, dear, dear... this sounds like a political matter, Mrs Morrow. I don't think I should interfere in this without back up.

PEGGY: Look, just tell him to get out.

WILY: This is bloody stupid.

PEGGY: You keep out of it.

WILY: There was no need to get them lot involved.

PEGGY: It'll give them something to do for a change.

Willy sits down and starts to eat. The Officer goes over to Peggy and whispers.

OFFICER: Mrs Morrow, I'll have to phone the station and see what can be done.

PEGGY:	Can't you just break down the door and throw him out?
OFFICER:	I'll need to speak to my superiors before any action of that kind can be taken.
PEGGY:	I should have known.
OFFICER:	Can I just take down a few details to make sure I've got the story straight?
PEGGY:	Bloody hell!
OFFICER:	Right. So your son, Kyle. Is that correct? Has barricaded himself into his room and refuses to leave the house even though you want him out?
PEGGY:	That's correct.
OFFICER:	And he pays rent but there's no tenancy agreement?
PEGGY:	Correct.
OFFICER:	Can I just ask why you want him out of the house?
PEGGY:	Because he's a… a queer.
OFFICER:	Oh. I see. I completely understand now, Mrs Morrow. I wouldn't want to be sharing my living space with a degenerate either. I'll just radio from the car and see what can be done.

He exits.

WILY: Don't you think you're taking this a bit too far?

PEGGY: No one gets the better of me.

WILY: No one's trying to.

PEGGY: Then why doesn't he leave?

WILY: Because he loves you, woman.

PEGGY: If he loved me he'd stop doing the things he does.

WILY: Like what? Standing up to you? I should have done it years ago.

PEGGY: Ha! You couldn't stand up to a fuckin' teletubby. You're a weakling.

WILY: We all can't be as hard as you, Peggy. Or as cruel.

PEGGY: Yeah well sometimes you need to be cruel to be kind.

WILY: If he's gay, he's gay. You can't change that.

PEGGY: He can choose not to act on it.

WILY: Like a priest, you mean?

PEGGY: Yes, like a bloody priest.

WILY: Well, well. Peggy Morrow, the biggest mouthpiece for the Protestant Church in the whole of Northern Ireland, advocating that her son live like a Catholic priest. What would her dearest Reverend McMillan have to say about that?

PEGGY: Fuck off and stop being so stupid.

WILY: You're the one who's being stupid. Nobody else, Peggy. Just you.

Officer Kildare returns.

OFFICER: My superiors say there's nothing they can do, Mrs Morrow.

WILY: (*To Peggy*) I'm off to work. This better be sorted out before I get back.

PEGGY: Since when have you started to give the orders around here?

Willy exits.

PEGGY: So now what?

OFFICER: My superiors suggest that you and your son sit down at a table and try to come to some kind of agreement.

PEGGY: I will never sit at the same table as dirty perverts.

OFFICER: I'm on your side where that is concerned, Mrs Morrow.

PEGGY: Then why don't you do something about it?

OFFICER: I can't. The RUC have to be seen to be impartial, Mrs Morrow. Though if it was up to me personally, I'd have every queer castrated. (*Whispering*) Would you like me to get the paramilitaries involved? They might be able to do something about it. We're powerless in these situations.

PEGGY: Is there any situation where you're not powerless?

OFFICER: There's no need to be like that.

PEGGY: Well, if you can't help me there's no point in hanging around here. Surely there's other things you could be doing?

OFFICER: No, actually. Since the peace there's been nothing much to do. All our overtime has been cut.

PEGGY: What a shame.

OFFICER: I relied on that overtime to pay for my scuba diving lessons. Now it looks like I'll have to give them up.

PEGGY: I wouldn't worry if I were you. This peace thing won't last.

OFFICER: I hope you're right. The sooner things get back to normal here the better.

He exits. Peggy goes to get a drink of vodka but the bottle is empty. She looks in her purse, grabs her coat and exits.

Seven

Afternoon. A terrorist, wearing a balaclava and combats, breaks into the house. Taking an aerosol spray from his pocket he starts to vandalise the walls: Faggots spread Aids; Ulster says No to Queers; Gays Out.

KYLE: Hallo, who's there? Come on, who is it?

The terrorist drums on Kyle's bedroom door with his hands. The drumming grows louder and louder. It sounds as threatening as the Lambeg drums. Kyle is frightened and moves back to his bed.

Eight

Evening. Peggy is sitting on the settee, drinking and smoking. Kyle sits on his bed holding his stomach. There is a knock at the front door. Peggy answers it. Kyle runs over to the bedroom door and presses his ear against it. Peggy opens the front door to Donal.

DONAL: Hello, Mrs Morrow.

PEGGY: Well, if it isn't Donal from Ardglass.

DONAL: Is Kyle in? I've been ringing all day but no-one's answering.

PEGGY: You better come in then and find out why.

Donal enters. He notices the graffiti on the walls.

DONAL: What's happened Mrs Morrow?

PEGGY: Sit down, Donal.

DONAL: Is Kyle okay?

PEGGY: Sit down, Donal.

DONAL: Where is he?

PEGGY: Sit down. You and I need to have a little chat.

Donal sits.

PEGGY: As you can see, my house has been sullied and desecrated.

DONAL: Is Kyle okay?

PEGGY: He's on hunger strike.

DONAL: (*Laughing nervously*) What?

PEGGY: He's barricaded himself into his room and gone on hunger strike.

DONAL: You're having me on, right?

PEGGY: He's told me about your dirty little secret.

DONAL: Oh...

PEGGY: Don't look so frightened. I'm not going to kneecap you. I just want you to persuade him to leave. I don't care what the two of you get up to, as long as it's not in my house.

DONAL: You told him to leave?

PEGGY: Yes, like any normal parent would.

DONAL: Not all parents react that strongly, Mrs Morrow.

PEGGY: I suppose yours didn't.

DONAL: No, they didn't.

PEGGY: Well, you must have extraordinary parents, Donal.

DONAL: No. Just ones that care.

PEGGY:	Look, Donal! Are you going to have a word with him or not?
DONAL:	I don't know if I should interfere. It's between you and him.
PEGGY:	If he loves you as much as he says he loves you, then he'll listen.
DONAL:	He said he loved me? (*Peggy nods.*) Okay. I suppose I can try.

Donal and Peggy go over to the door.

DONAL:	Kyle!
KYLE:	Fuck sake, I'm not deaf.
DONAL:	What are you playing at?
KYLE:	I wouldn't say that starving myself was playing at anything.
DONAL:	Of course you're not starving yourself. Don't be daft.
KYLE:	If you call one bite of a mouldy, old pizza in twenty-four hours not starving yourself, then I guess I'm not.
DONAL:	Why don't you just leave?
KYLE:	It's a matter of principles.
DONAL:	What good are principles when your stomach is shrivelling up?

KYLE: A man has to take a stand at some point in his life.

DONAL: There's better ways of doing it. You're just making matters worse.

KYLE: Things have to get worse before they get better, so they say.

DONAL: Okay but what is it you want?

KYLE: Well, I'm glad you've brought that subject up, Donal coz I've now got a few demands for Mommie Dearest.

PEGGY: You can demand all you like son, but it doesn't mean they'll be met.

KYLE: One, I want an apology and her agreement to let me stay in the house. Two, I want her to say that she'll try and accept me for who I am and what I am. Three, I want her to acknowledge my right to associate with whoever I wish no matter what their religion or sexual orientation. Four, I want her to agree to let you stay over whenever I want you to. And five, I want the right not to do housework.

PEGGY: You cheeky, lazy good-for-nothing little bastard.

KYLE: I thought you'd like that.

PEGGY: Hell will freeze over before I agree to any of that crap.

KYLE: Well I'm not moving from here or eating another crumb until you do.

DONAL: Wise up, Kyle. Stop messing around.

KYLE: I'm serious. I want her to see sense. I want her to see that she still has a son who loves her and refuses to give up on her, even though she's a stubborn, old, bigoted bitch.

PEGGY: This stubborn, old, bigoted bitch can't love a son who goes against everything she stands for.

KYLE: Oh, so you don't love me now. Is that how it is?

PEGGY: Yes!

Pause. She goes and pours herself a vodka and sits down on the settee.

DONAL: Kyle, look. I've put the deposit down on the flat now. You don't need to do this. You'll be better off without her.

KYLE: I can't give in. Not now.

DONAL: You can't force her into accepting you. These things take time.

KYLE: I prefer a more active role. Sitting doing nothing while others make up their minds is not for me.

DONAL: It won't quicken the process.

KYLE: Look, I know my own Ma. This is the only way. She respects those who fight, and so do I.

Pause.

DONAL: (*Intimately*) Kyle, we could be sitting in our own flat right now. Doing what we want. Free. Just the two of us in our little sanctuary. Don't you want that?

KYLE: This is more important.

Donal is hurt.

KYLE: Donal?

Donal doesn't answer. He walks over to Peggy.

DONAL: You deserve each other.

He exits, almost knocking Willy over as he enters.

WILY: Who was that?

PEGGY: Saint fucking Patrick.

He sees the graffiti.

WILY: What in God's name has happened here?

71

PEGGY: What does it look like?

WILY: Those fuckin' hoodlums!

PEGGY: What did you expect? People round here don't want perverts living near them. And I can't say I blame them.

WILY: So you think this is okay, do you?

PEGGY: I didn't say that.

WILY: You'd take their side before your own son's?

PEGGY: In this matter, yes.

WILY: You're a sad woman, Peggy.

PEGGY: He's in the wrong.

WILY: And vandalising someone's house is right?

PEGGY: Of course it's not. That's why I want him out, before we're bombed out.

WILY: This is madness.

PEGGY: Don't blame me. It's his fault.

WILY: He's not still in that room, is he? Ach, for God's sake. This has gone too far. Has he eaten yet?

Peggy shrugs her shoulders. Willy marches over to the bedroom door.

72

WILY: Hay son, come out and get something to eat. You'll be making yourself ill if you don't.

KYLE: Tell her that.

PEGGY: (*To Kyle*) It's your choice.

WILY: Shut your mouth, woman. Look son, if I make you some beans and toast will you eat it?

KYLE: No, Da. I can't.

Kyle, upset, goes to his bed and puts on his headphones.

WILY: I'm making you something to eat and you're bloody well going to eat it.

He heads towards the kitchen. Peggy obstructs his path.

PEGGY: And what do you think you're doing?

WILY: He has to eat something, even if I have to ram it down his throat.

PEGGY: Oh no, sonny Jim. He's made his bed, now he can lie in it.

WILY: You'd let your own son starve?

PEGGY: He'll give in before that happens, believe me.

WILY: And if he doesn't?

PEGGY: He will.

WILY: Aren't you tired of all this fighting? We should be having a bit of peace at our age.

PEGGY: You've had nothing but peace. Not once have you had to lift your hand when it needed to be lifted.

WILY: That's because you always got there first.

PEGGY: It's because you didn't have the balls.

WILY: I'm making Kyle something to eat, and that's the end of it.

PEGGY: I wouldn't if I were you.

WILY: Your bullying has killed one child. I'm not letting you do it again.

Peggy slaps him hard across the face.

WILY: She took those tablets because of you, Peggy.

PEGGY: She took them because she was weak.

WILY: You kicked any strength she had outta her.

PEGGY: I loved her.

WILY: Then why wouldn't you let her and the Robinson boy marry?

Pause.

PEGGY: He wasn't right for her.

WILY: She loved him, that's all that mattered.

PEGGY: She was too good for him.

WILY: You could have swallowed your pride for once.

PEGGY: I couldn't.

WILY: You murdered my little girl, Peggy and I'll never forgive you for that.

He walks towards the door of the kitchen.

PEGGY: *MY* little girl. You mean, *my* little girl.

Willy stops.

WILY: That's the first time in twenty years you've said that to me, Peggy. And it's the last time.

He walks towards the bedroom.

PEGGY: Where are you going?

Willy doesn't answer. He enters the bedroom. Peggy sits down on the settee and lights up a cigarette. She is drained. After a few minutes, Willy comes out with a suitcase. He walks over to Kyle's room.

WILY: Kyle? Kyle!

KYLE:	What?
WILY:	I'm leaving son. I want you to come with me.
KYLE:	What are you talking about?
WILY:	I'm leaving – for good.
KYLE:	Why? What's happened?
WILY:	I should have done it years ago.
KYLE:	Don't be fucking stupid.
WILY:	Son, I'm going. I've made up my mind.
KYLE:	But she needs you.
WILY:	Your Ma's the big woman. She needs no one.
KYLE:	Da, don't go.
WILY:	It's too late. Now come on, before she kills you as well.
KYLE:	No. I'll stay.
WILY:	Son, please.
KYLE:	I can't.
WILY:	(*Pause*) If you need me I'll be at your Uncle Dave's.

Willy turns and exits.

KYLE: Ma? Ma, are you okay?

Nine

Midnight. Peggy is lying drunk on the settee. Snow starts falling and Nelson Eddy re-appears singing the beginning of Indian Love Call. *She approaches Peggy.*

PEGGY: Oh God, not again.

NELSON: Peggy, you're a treasure. Now come on, sit up.

Nelson tries to help Peggy into a sitting position.

PEGGY: Get your filthy hands off me!

NELSON: A girl of your age should not be seen lying flat on her face in a drunken stupor.

PEGGY: Fuck off!

NELSON: (*Laughing*) Of all the queens that ever lived, I had to pick you.

PEGGY: Get out of my house!

NELSON: Your hospitality is boundless.

PEGGY: Look, take your piss clever talk somewhere else and leave me alone, will ya? And stop prowling around my house.

NELSON: Doesn't Kyle live here as well?

PEGGY: Don't start.

NELSON: Hasn't he got a valid claim to this house?

PEGGY: It's my house!

NELSON: And Kyle's home.

PEGGY: It's none of your business.

NELSON: But you asked for my help.

PEGGY: Like fuck.

NELSON: I think you did, dearest darling. Now stop fighting the truth and let's have some fun. Here put these on.

She hands Peggy the dress and the wig. Peggy stares at them.

NELSON: Don't you want to be Jeanette again?

PEGGY: No I do not.

NELSON: If you're a good girl, you can have her longer this time.

PEGGY: (*Sarcastically*) You're so kind.

NELSON: Thank you. Generosity is a rule we should all abide by.

PEGGY: Look, I'm not listening to you anymore. You don't even exist. My drunken mind has created you.

NELSON: And why would it do that?

Pause.

PEGGY: Look, just piss off back to where you came from. I've got a headache.

NELSON: Not just yet, Peggy. There's someone I think you need to speak to.

Jim Robinson appears. His knees have been smashed. There is a gunshot wound in his head and his face is covered with blood.

JIM: Peggy!

PEGGY: Jim?

JIM: Give us a hand luv.

PEGGY: (*To Nelson*) Is this some kind of sick joke?

NELSON: You tell me.

JIM: Peggy luv, help us out will ya?

Peggy runs over to Jim and helps him up onto the settee.

PEGGY: Are you alright, Jim?

JIM: Have never been better.

PEGGY: But...?

She looks at the hole in his head and his knees.

JIM: Oh this. It's only a few scratches.

PEGGY: But there's a hole in your head the size of Lough Neagh.

JIM: Jesus, so that's what did it.

80

He laughs.

PEGGY: Jim, are you really… you know… dead?

JIM: Well if I'm not, it's the biggest bloody headache I've ever had.

PEGGY: Do you want a cup of tea?

JIM: I'd rather have a scotch.

PEGGY: I should have known.

NELSON: I'll get it, Peggy. You stay here and have a chat.

JIM: Boy you've put on a bit of weight since I saw you last, Peggy. It doesn't suit you.

PEGGY: You're not looking too grand yourself.

JIM: That's the Peggy I remember. Give as good as she gets.

PEGGY: Why are you here, Jim?

JIM: To have a wee word in your ear about your son.

Nelson hands him the drink.

PEGGY: Since when has the head of the 32nd battalion taken an interest in domestic affairs?

JIM: It is a political situation, Peggy.

81

PEGGY: And how's that?

JIM: Homosexuality is antithetical to the Protestant cause.

PEGGY: That's a big word, Jim. Having your brains blown out seems to have improved your mind.

JIM: Don't get smart, Peggy.

PEGGY: Well I can't see how my son being queer can affect the cause.

JIM: If word gets out about his hunger strike it could have devastating affects on our popularity. Look at what the H Block strikes did. They set us back twenty years. We can't take that risk again.

PEGGY: This has got nothing to do with the Troubles, Jim. So what's your problem?

JIM: Homosexuality is like cancer, Peggy. One cell soon multiples into thousands and before you know it the whole body has been ravaged by it. It could weaken our hold.

Pause.

PEGGY: So what are you suggesting?

JIM: I'm not suggesting, Peggy. I'm telling you. Get him to give up the hunger strike and

	leave the area. Or let our lot sort him out for you.
PEGGY:	That's my son, Jim.
JIM:	What's more important? Him or Ulster? *(Pause.)* You let one child die, Peggy. What difference does another make?
PEGGY:	You disgust me.
JIM:	I didn't always. I remember the days when you couldn't get enough of me; when you needed a real man instead of that chicken livered doormat of a husband of yours.
PEGGY:	Willy's twice the man you'll ever be.

Jim laughs.

JIM:	You don't mean that Peggy.
PEGGY:	Oh, I mean it Jim. I only wish I'd seen it a long time ago.
JIM:	I could still make you feel like a real woman, Peggy. Come on. One last time before I...

Jim forces himself onto Peggy. She pushes him off.

PEGGY:	Go to hell, Jim.
JIM:	One last fuck for Ulster! Come on, Peggy. One last good hard fuck for Ulster!

NELSON: Time to meet your maker, Jim.

Nelson lifts Jim and carries him off. Peggy sees the dress on the floor, puts it on and sings, Lover Come back to me (Hammerstein II & Romberg). Nelson re-enters after the song.

NELSON: Feel better, dearest? (*Peggy smiles*) There's nothing like a good song to lift your spirits.

PEGGY: You remind me of what Willy was like, do you know that? He has a good voice as well, so he does. Deeper than yours. He used to sing to me when we were courting. Sounds corny now, but then it was very romantic. We both lived for the cinema, you know. Especially the musicals. We'd see the same film over and over again until we had learned all the words to all the songs. Then we'd come home and act out the scenes.

NELSON: It was a gay time, that's for sure.

Peggy looks at Nelson suspiciously.

PEGGY: It was... while it lasted.

NELSON: It's still there, Peggy. Inside you. Waiting to burst out like a firecracker.

PEGGY: You've brought it back, but this isn't real. It's just day-dreaming.

NELSON: Dreams are the gateway to a better reality, darling. You need to learn how to use them.

PEGGY: Can you teach me?

NELSON: You're half way there already.

Peggy smiles.

PEGGY: If I weren't a married woman I could fall for you. You're the only one who brings a smile to my face these days.

NELSON: Kyle could make you smile, if you let him. And so could Willy.

PEGGY: They used to.

NELSON: So what happened?

PEGGY: Life.

Pause.

NELSON: Peggy, you've got a lot to smile about if you'd just open your eyes. You've got a son who loves you very much and needs your support. That's something.

PEGGY: How can I support him when he goes against everything I believe in?

NELSON: And what do you believe in, Peggy?

PEGGY: In God. In the Protestant faith.

NELSON: Then you should also believe in 'thou shalt not lie', 'thou shalt not commit adultery'. 'Do not judge others so that you will not be judged.'

PEGGY: Alright, alright! You've said what you planned to say now you can piss off!

NELSON: Not until you agree to speak to Kyle... like a mother.

PEGGY: I've nothing to say.

NELSON: Do you want him to die? (*Pause.*) Well, do you?

PEGGY: No.

NELSON: Then you'll have to speak to him.

PEGGY: I don't know what to say.

NELSON: Since when have you been lost for words, Peggy Morrow?

Ten

The following day. Kyle is lying on top of his bed, holding his stomach. He's in pain. Peggy stands with her ear to the bedroom door looking concerned. Suddenly, she knocks.

PEGGY: Kyle, are you alright?

KYLE: I'm fine.

PEGGY: I think you should eat something.

KYLE: Only if you allow me to stay.

PEGGY: I think we should try and reach a compromise.

KYLE: How?

PEGGY: If you agree to have a chat with Reverend McMillan, I'll let you stay.

KYLE: That's not a compromise, that's a fucking ultimatum.

PEGGY: I'm trying to find a solution here.

KYLE: You'll have to try harder then.

PEGGY: Can't you shift just a little?

KYLE: It sounds like I'm the one who's expected to do all the shifting.

PEGGY: It's the best I can do at this moment in time.

87

KYLE: Why would I want to have a chat with that raving, lunatic anyway?

PEGGY: He might be able to help... make you see that, well... maybe you're not gay.

KYLE: Ma, I'm gay!

PEGGY: But you're young. It could be a phase.

KYLE: I'm gay, for Christ's sake! I'm in love with Donal. Donal is in love with me. We're two men. Therefore, I'm gay.

PEGGY: Look, when I was a young girl I used to know this woman called Maisie. Maisie only ever wore men's suits that she'd picked up at Smithfield's and her hair was always greased back like Marlene Deitrich. She used to terrorize the young girls on our street by whistling at them. Then she'd let out this cackle of a laugh like a banshee. All the girls hated her, but I was mesmerized. I thought I loved her... but it was a childish love. It wasn't a sexual love. I didn't know what that was until I met your Da. Maybe you just need to meet the right wee girl.

KYLE: For God's sake, I'm gay.

PEGGY: You might grow out of it.

KYLE: Look, I'm queer. Just accept it.

PEGGY: Alright, but even if you are, maybe Reverend McMillan can help you change. You could get involved in the church or something.

Kyle is exasperated.

KYLE: I LIKE SCREWING OTHER MEN AND I'LL ALWAYS LIKE SCREWING OTHER MEN. Now does that satisfy you?

Peggy is stunned.

PEGGY: You're disgusting. I can't believe you're my son.

KYLE: It's the way I am.

Pause.

PEGGY: Look, won't you at least give McMillan one chance?

KYLE: Ma, even if I thought I could change, I wouldn't want to. I'm proud to be gay. And from now on I'm gonna fight for the right to be gay and for the rights of others to be gay in this God forsaken country.

PEGGY: You're even beginning to sound like a fenian.

KYLE: Well, I'm beginning to understand how they felt.

89

PEGGY: You're no son of mine then.

Peggy throws her coat on and exits. Kyle goes back to bed, still in pain and getting weaker. He falls asleep and starts dreaming. Nelson appears and opens his bedroom window. A terrorist, wearing a balaclava climbs into the room. He goes over to Kyle and wakes him.

KYLE: Jesus!

The terrorist places his hand over Kyle's mouth.

TERRORIST: Shush. Bloody hell, keep quiet. I'm not going to hurt you. I'm here to help. Now are you going to keep that mouth shut? (Kyle nods.) Good.

He removes his hand.

KYLE: Help!

The terrorist covers Kyle's mouth again.

TERRORIST: Listen, if you try that again I'll have to gag you, alright? Now I'm not here to hurt you, so trust me.

He pulls his hands away.

KYLE: Who are you and what do you want?

TERRORIST: I'm a soldier of the I.Q.L.A.

KYLE: The what?

TERRORIST: (*With comic pride*) The Irish Queer
Liberation Army.

He holds out his hand. Kyle laughs.

KYLE: Yeah, and I'm a member of the Salvation
Army.

TERRORIST: No, it's the truth. We're a newly formed
organisation of men and women dedicated
to the cause - complete liberation of all
queers in Ireland. We use whatever means
are necessary to secure our rights to self
determination.

KYLE: You're serious?

TERRORIST: Of course I'm bloody serious. Don't you think
it's about time the people in this country
were forced to recognise the rights of us
Queers?

KYLE: And what rights are those?

TERRORIST: We want the right to be able to live without
someone's boot pressing down on our
throats.

KYLE: Okay, okay, but can't you think of a more
creative way of doing it? Like, like painting
the city hall pink or running up and down
the Shankill and the Falls naked with 'love
me' painted on your arse cheeks.

91

TERRORIST:	That'id really help our cause.
KYLE:	Of course it would. Give people something to laugh about for a change.
TERRORIST:	The armalite is the only language the people of this island recognise.
KYLE:	You actually kill people then?
TERRORIST:	I don't know many terrorist groups who only shout abuse, do you?
KYLE:	I don't know many terrorist groups who wear combats as a fashion statement either.
TERRORIST:	We wear them because they're practical for the kind of work we do.
KYLE:	You wear them because you think it makes you look good, admit it?
TERRORIST:	Look, I'll admit that a pair of combats can make any old queen look half-decent, but that is not why we wear them. Terrorism is a messy business and combats are the most durable of trousers.
KYLE:	Don't you think there's enough gangsters in this country without us joining them?
TERRORIST:	We're not like the others. Our cause is valid because it concerns fundamental issues of

human nature and not just squabbles over a piece of land.

KYLE: You can find an excuse for any cause, that's why killing innocent people in the name of one is ridiculous.

TERRORIST: We do not kill innocent people. Only homophobes and bigots.

KYLE: If you killed every homophobe and bigot in this country there'd be no one left.

TERRORIST: Us queers would be left.

KYLE: What, all twelve of us?

TERRORIST: Ha, bloody ha.

KYLE: Look, I admire your convictions. An Ulster inhabited only by queers would certainly be an improvement, but killing is not the answer. It doesn't work.

TERRORIST: It's worked for everyone else.

KYLE: Forty years of pain and suffering hasn't worked for anyone.

TERRORIST: It's worked for those who now sit in positions of power.

KYLE: It may seem that way.

TERRORIST:	The end justifies the means. Terrorism works.
KYLE:	The end never justifies the means, because there never is an end. Only consequences.
TERRORIST:	How do you mean?
KYLE:	You're not very bright are you?
TERRORIST:	Look, I've come here to help you, not to be insulted.
KYLE:	How can you help me?
TERRORIST:	With this situation, your mother.
KYLE:	How did you know about that?
TERRORIST:	The closet can sometimes provide us with a very useful peephole onto the world, comrade.
KYLE:	So I'm a comrade, am I?
TERRORIST:	You're queer, aren't you?
KYLE:	Very much so.
TERRORIST:	Well then. I'm here to offer you support and advice.
KYLE:	And what's your advice?
TERRORIST:	Let us sort her out for you.
KYLE:	How?

TERRORIST: With a little scare.

KYLE: That's my Ma you're talking about.

TERRORIST: What good's a Ma who doesn't let her son be who he wants to be?

KYLE: More good than a dead one.

TERRORIST: We're not talking about killing her, only scaring her.

KYLE: (*Sarcastically*) Oh, that's okay then.

TERRORIST: So you'll let us do it?

KYLE: Of course not, you dickhead.

TERRORIST: There's no need to be rude. We're only trying to stop you from starving yourself.

KYLE: Thanks, but I'll be fine.

TERRORIST: Are you sure? You don't look too fine to me.

KYLE: Look, I don't need your kind of help.

TERRORIST: Your Ma is a bigot and a homophobe. She needs to be taught a lesson or two.

KYLE: And you think you could teach her?

TERRORIST: Well, yes.

KYLE: She'd eat you up like a potato farl.

TERRORIST: Not with a gun to her head.

KYLE: That wouldn't stop her. Her skin is bullet proof.

TERRORIST: Look, I know she's your Ma and all, but we queers have to stick together. We're the only real family you've got.

KYLE: It takes more than a common love of fucking other men to bond a family.

TERRORIST: I take it you don't want our help then?

KYLE: Definitely not.

TERRORIST: You're making a big mistake.

KYLE: Somehow I doubt it.

TERRORIST: I'll go then.

KYLE: You do that.

The terrorist walks disappointedly towards the window.

KYLE: Hold on a minute. There is something you could do to help.

TERRORIST: What?

KYLE: Come here.

He goes over to Kyle who unzips the terrorist's flies.

KYLE: I'm dying for something to eat. You don't mind, do you?

TERRORIST: Anything to help a comrade.

The terrorist removes his balaclava.

KYLE: Donal!

DONAL: I leave you for one day and already you're copping off with another man.

KYLE: I didn't mean it. I'm sorry. I don't know what I'm doing.

DONAL: (*Laughing*) Kyle, relax. It's only a dream. I understand.

KYLE: What's going on? Why are you here?

DONAL: To say I'm sorry.

KYLE: But it's me who should be saying sorry.

DONAL: No.

KYLE: She's not more important.

DONAL: You can't give up now. I have it on good authority that things are about to change.

KYLE: But I've had enough. My stomach aches, my vision's blurred and my mind is all over the place.

DONAL: You have to keep going.

KYLE: Are you sure?

DONAL: Yes, it won't be long now. Here.

Donal kisses him.

KYLE: Maybe you should start getting that flat ready. Paint a few walls or something.

DONAL: I already have.

Lights.

Eleven

Later. Peggy enters singing The Sash. She's drunk. She goes to Kyle's door. Kyle is asleep, dreaming of Donal.

PEGGY: Kyle! Kyle! Come out and fight like a man! Kyle! Kyle!

She sits down on the stairs and passes out. Nelson enters carrying a tray with tea. She puts it down on the table and then stands at the front door. There's a knock. Peggy wakes.

NELSON: Aren't you going to answer that, my beauty?

PEGGY: Answer it yourself.

NELSON: It's your house as you keep telling me. You won't be disappointed.

PEGGY: Is it Willy? (*She answers the door. It's Reverend McMillan.*) Oh my God, it's you. I can't believe it. (*She drops to her knees.*)

MCMILLAN: Get off your knees, woman. I'm only a man, an ordinary man.

PEGGY: I can't believe it. I'm so happy.

MCMILLAN: I'm no false idol so please don't treat me as such.

PEGGY: I'm sorry. I'm sorry. You're so right, Reverend McMillan. Please come in.

MCMILLAN: Do you mind if a dear friend of mine joined us?

PEGGY: Oh no, not at all.

MCMILLAN: You're a fine Christian woman, Mrs Morrow.

From behind McMillan a frail, tiny Cardinal Dainty appears. Peggy is shocked.

MCMILLAN: This is Cardinal Dainty.

PEGGY: Yes, I know who it is.

MCMILLAN: Is there a problem?

PEGGY: I'm just... shocked to see you two... (together) I thought you hated each other.

MCMILLAN: We are men of God. We do not hate.

PEGGY: But he stands for everything you're against.

CARDINAL: Appearances can be deceiving, Mrs Morrow.

PEGGY: You'd know all about that.

MCMILLAN: Now, now Mrs Morrow. Ye must put your prejudices to one side, at least until we've left.

PEGGY: But he's a figurehead for the very thing we're opposed to.

MCMILLAN: In the world of politics opposition is not a reality, but a tool. Now are ye going to offer us a seat woman, or do we have to stand all night?

PEGGY: No, of course not. Please sit down.

MCMILLAN: After you, Cardinal.

CARDINAL: Why thank you, Reverend.

They sit.

PEGGY: Would you like a cup of tea, Reverend?

MCMILLAN: That's very kind of you, Mrs Morrow. God's work is thirsty work.

Peggy heads towards the kitchen. Nelson points out the tea already on the table.

CARDINAL: Do you have any sherry perchance?

PEGGY: No.

CARDINAL: Oh, tea is fine then.

PEGGY: Sugar, Reverend?

CARDINAL: Five please.

She throws the spoonfuls of sugar into his cup.

PEGGY: Reverend?

MCMILLAN: Six please. (*He takes a sip.*) That's a quare cup of tea, Mrs Morrow.

101

PEGGY: Thank you.

MCMILLAN: Now you're probably wondering why we're here.

PEGGY: You've heard about Kyle, I take it.

MCMILLAN: Indeed. We've come to offer you our full support for the stand you're taking against him and his terrible sin.

PEGGY: But it's difficult, Reverend. He's starving himself to death. I don't know if I can keep going, so I don't.

MCMILLAN: Just remember, you have RIGHT on your side. Homosexuality is wrong and unnatural. It needs to be wiped off the face of the earth, just like terrorism. And remember Mrs Morrow, it was Adam and Eve, not Adam and Steve.

McMillan and the Cardinal burst out laughing like two schoolboys.

MCMILLAN: That one always gets me. Don't ye think it's funny, Mrs Morrow?

PEGGY: I used to.

CARDINAL: Now, now. You can't let all of this destroy your sense of humour.

MCMILLAN: Sometimes it's all a person can have left.

PEGGY: I'd rather lose that than my son.

MCMILLAN: You can't give in now... Peggy. If ye do, ye'll be encouraging every pervert in Ulster to crawl out of the woodwork.

PEGGY: But I love my son.

MCMILLAN: So do we.

CARDINAL: It's homosexual acts we hate. Not the homosexual. He needs our love and support, and encouragement to give up his aberrant ways. And this is what you're doing.

PEGGY: But he might die?

MCMILLAN: Sometimes sacrifices are necessary for the greater good.

PEGGY: But surely you don't want him to become a martyr, because that is what will happen.

MCMILLAN: Only the church can decide who becomes a martyr, and on this we're both agreed to do everything in our power to stop it happening. Aren't we, Cardinal?

CARDINAL: Most certainly, Reverend.

PEGGY: But what am I to do?

MCMILLAN: Whatever God asks of ye.

PEGGY: I'm not sure if I know what he wants.

MCMILLAN: He wants you to remain firm in your resolve to get your son to leave the house and renounce his filthy ways.

CARDINAL: It's the only way, Mrs Morrow, of keeping the Province clean of this disease.

PEGGY: I don't know if I'm strong enough.

MCMILLAN: Of course you are, woman. You're a Presbyterian!

CARDINAL: And you aren't alone in this. You have the backing of both churches.

MCMILLAN: And that privilege isn't accorded to many people, Mrs Morrow. Now where is this son of yours? I'd like a word.

PEGGY: Uhm... he's behind there.

All three move over to Kyle's room.

MCMILLAN: Hallo in there. Can you hear me? This is the Reverend McMillan. Can you hear me?

KYLE: I'm not deaf.

MCMILLAN: We want a little chat.

KYLE: About what?

MCMILLAN: About salvation. Your salvation.

KYLE: Go fuck yourself.

PEGGY: Kyle!

Cardinal crosses himself.

MCMILLAN: It's okay, Mrs Morrow. As God's minister I am used to the language of heathens. Now listen here, young man. I have not come here to condemn or to ridicule. I have come to help you. I simply want to save you from the pits of hell.

KYLE: I'd rather burn in Hell than listen to you, thanks very much.

MCMILLAN: May the lord have mercy on ye. Ye do not know what ye say.

KYLE: Piss off, you ranting old man.

PEGGY: Kyle, watch your mouth.

MCMILLAN: His words have no effect on me, Mrs Morrow.

KYLE: Then you won't mind me telling you to get the fuck out of this house coz I'm not interested in your scare mongering.

MCMILLAN: I am not trying to scare ye. I am trying to show you the light. To help you take the right path instead of following the one to eternal damnation.

KYLE: Bollocks!

MCMILLAN: Leviticus 20:13. If a man lie with mankind,
             as he lieth with a woman, both of them
             have committed an abomination.

KYLE: Love thy neighbour as thyself. Matthew
             19:19

CARDINAL: He's got you there, Reverend.

MCMILLAN: Now listen here. God has smitten you lot
             with one plague, isn't that enough to
             convince you that what you're doing is
             wrong?

KYLE: Go stick your head up your arse!

MCMILLAN: Your mind is corrupted, young man.

KYLE: Corruption comes in many forms,
             Reverend, but usually in the guise of virtue
             and morality. What's it like to be so
             virtuous?

*The Cardinal sniggers and McMillan throws him a look of
daggers.*

MCMILLAN: You're an insolent little bugger.

PEGGY: Now hold on a minute…

MCMILLAN: I hope your stomach shrivels to the size of
             a peanut.

PEGGY: Reverend...

MCMILLAN: I hope your bones tear through your flesh.

PEGGY: There's no need for that.

CARDINAL: The Reverend knows what he's doing.

MCMILLAN: You're not fit for life.

PEGGY: Now hold on.

MCMILLAN: He's a miscreant. A pervert.

PEGGY: That's enough.

MCMILLAN: A paedophile.

PEGGY: He might like other men, but he's no child molester.

MCMILLAN: He doesn't deserve to live. The sooner you get rid of him the better.

PEGGY: I'm not standing for that!

MCMILLAN: May I remind you who I am, Mrs Morrow.

PEGGY: I don't care who you are. No one speaks to my son like that, except me. Now piss off!

MCMILLAN: Wash your mouth, woman, you are talking to the Reverend McMillan!

PEGGY: And you are talking to Mrs Peggy Morrow. So bugger off!

CARDINAL: We are only doing God's good work, Mrs Morrow.

PEGGY: Then take him with you as well. Go on, fuck off.

Nelson who has been watching the above scene, opens the door for Peggy. Peggy pushes the Cardinal out.

MCMILLAN: You'll only have yourself to blame, Mrs Morrow, when you find your house has been turned into a Sodom & Gomorrah. Be warned.

He exits. Nelson slams the door shut. She smiles at Peggy.

PEGGY: And you can piss off as well.

Peggy goes to the stairs and sits down. She's confused, concerned and falls back to sleep.

Twelve

Morning. Kyle lies asleep on bed. Willy appears at the window wearing his postman's uniform and carrying a bulging post sack. He opens the window and climbs through clumsily. He falls onto the bedroom floor. Kyle wakens.

KYLE: Da?

WILY: Son, how are you keeping?

KYLE: Okay, just a little weak.

WILY: We'll soon have you sorted out. Here...

He empties the contents of his post sack onto the floor – loads of provisions.

WILY: A feast. A bloody, big feast.

KYLE: Did you bring any water?

WILY: Yeah. It's here somewhere.

Willy finds a bottle of water and gives it to Kyle. Kyle tries to unscrew it but can't manage. Willy does it for him, looking worried. Kyle drinks from the bottle.

KYLE: That's better.

WILY: Now how about something to eat? I've got some of those onion beejees that you like.

KYLE: Bhaji's, da.

WILY: What?

109

.

KYLE: Onion bhaji.

WILY: Well whatever they are. Here.

KYLE: I can't eat them.

WILY: What's wrong with them?

KYLE: Nothing. I can't eat anything. It wouldn't be right.

WILY: But you'll get sick. Look at the state of you already.

KYLE: I'm fine. Now that I've had some water.

WILY: Son, you have to eat something, even if I have to force you.

KYLE: Come off it, Da. You've never forced me to do anything in your life before. You can't start now.

WILY: I'm not letting you get sick. I'm not letting another child…

Pause.

KYLE: That won't happen.

WILY: I know it won't because I won't let it happen.

Pause.

KYLE: Tell me what she was like, Da? Anne. I can't remember much about her, except her long red hair.

WILY: I'll tell you after you eat something.

KYLE: Did she take after you or Ma?

WILY: Son... there's something you should know.

KYLE: What?

Pause.

WILY: Anne was the sweetest girl that ever lived. Never had a bad word to say about anyone. Always put other people's feelings before her own.

KYLE: She took after you then.

WILY: Your Ma used to be sweet as well, son. Full of love. Always had a smile on her face.

KYLE: Come off it.

WILY: Don't you remember what she was like when you were a wean? All the singing and dancing she did around the house.

KYLE: Are you sure you're talking about Ma?

WILY: I remember one day in particular. You must have been about eight or nine. Your Ma had just come home from the hairdressers. She used to be so fussy about her appearance. Anyway, she was sitting in the kitchen with this new hairdo, that must have taken ages to do coz I'd never seen hair so high in my life. She was sitting having a cup of tea, afraid to move her head in case it wrecked the new hairstyle. And you came in. You went straight to the fridge took out a bottle of milk and shook it, thinking the top was still on it. It wasn't. And the milk flew everywhere, all over the kitchen floor, all over me and all over your Ma's new hairstyle. I've never seen something so tall fall so quickly.

KYLE: She must have killed me.

WILY: I thought you were a goner for sure, but you know what she did? She stood up and she laughed and she laughed and then she grabbed you by the hands and started to dance – right there in the middle of the floor, in all that milk with hair sticking to her face. That's the type of woman your Ma used to be.

KYLE: So what happened to her?

WILY: Anne and the Robinson boy. The Troubles. Who knows, son.

KYLE:	Did she ever tell you why she hated the Robinson lad so much?
WILY:	Just said he wasn't good enough for Anne.
KYLE:	And was he?
WILY:	I've never liked the Robinson's. They're a bad lot, but the son seemed ok and Anne was head over heals in love with him which, to me was all that mattered.
KYLE:	I still can't believe what happened.
WILY:	There's never a day goes past when I don't think about it, but you just have to get on with things.
KYLE:	I suppose so.

Pause.

WILY:	Will you have something to eat, son?
KYLE:	No, Da.
WILY:	But son…
KYLE:	Da. Don't you want to get the woman back who dances in milk with hair stuck to her face?
WILY:	That could take a long time.
KYLE:	Maybe not. You see, last night I had this dream. A terrorist broke into my room only

113

it wasn't a terrorist it was Donal and he told me to keep going, that things were going to change. He said it wouldn't be long now.

WILY: You were hallucinating, son.

KYLE: I know it sounds crazy Da, but don't you see? It's a sign. Something's happening with Ma. I just need to stick it out a bit longer.

WILY: You need something to eat, that's what you need.

KYLE: No.

Pause.

WILY: Is there nothing I can say that will make you change your mind?

KYLE: Afraid not.

WILY: God, you're your mother's son alright.

KYLE: How could it be any different? You were never here.

WILY: You don't think that's why you've turned out... you know? I can't stop thinking that I'm to blame. Maybe if I'd been around more, played football with you or taken you with me to play golf... It's my fault that you got too close to your mother, but

114

after Anne... well, I just didn't have it in me.

KYLE: You're here for me now. So that's all that matters.

WILY: Are you sure you won't have something to eat?

KYLE: Let's just see what happens.

Thirteen

Night. Peggy is pacing up and down the room in front of Kyle's door, looking extremely worried. Kyle lies on bed holding his stomach. Peggy goes to get a vodka, but changes her mind. She goes into the kitchen. Nelson appears, carrying a can of paint and a brush. She starts to paint over the graffiti. Peggy enters with a cup of tea.

NELSON: Ah, darling. There you are.

PEGGY: I thought you'd left for good this time.

NELSON: Without a big musical number, never!

Peggy is silent. She sits down.

NELSON: What's the matter?

PEGGY: As if you didn't know.

NELSON: Tell me.

PEGGY: You. And all the other things that have been going on around here. I don't understand any of it. I can't even trust my own eyes anymore. I think I'm heading for Purdysburn.

NELSON: (*Laughing*) Oh, Peggy! Madhouses are for the mad. You're saner than you've ever been.

PEGGY: Don't talk nonsense. I've never been more confused.

NELSON: Confusion is good.

PEGGY: But I feel seasick, as if the earth beneath my feet is made from water. I want it to be solid again. I want things back to normal. I want Willy back, and I want Kyle to be... well, not to be the way he is.

NELSON: Kyle is who he is. It's you who has to change.

PEGGY: I can't. It's too difficult. A person just can't wake up one morning and be someone else.

NELSON: They can if they want it bad enough.

PEGGY: Maybe in your world they can, but not in this real world.

NELSON: Just look at yourself for a minute. You've changed so much already, if only you'd allow yourself to recognise it.

PEGGY: My insides are doing somersaults. I can't bear it. I need a stable world to live in.

NELSON: Then why do you turn everything into a battlefield. (*Pause.*) You've got to let Kyle stay in the house, Peggy. You deserve a happy ending.

PEGGY: I want to... but what if I catch him and Donal... you know. I wouldn't be able to stand it.

117

NELSON: Just talk to him about it.

PEGGY: I'm afraid of what I'll say, what I'll hear.

NELSON: There's nothing to be afraid of. Surely you trust me by now?

Nelson jumps up and holds out her hand. She starts to sing the first verse of Ah, Sweet Mystery of Life (R.J. Young – V. Herbert). Peggy is reluctant at first, but then takes her hand. They repeat the song together. When it's finished they kiss passionately. Peggy feels Nelson's breasts. She pulls away in shock.

PEGGY: You're a woman!

NELSON: I use Ponds nourishment cream if that's what you mean?

PEGGY: You've got breasts.

NELSON: If that's all it takes to be a woman, then I guess I am.

PEGGY: It's disgusting.

NELSON: Love knows no boundaries.

PEGGY: You've tricked me.

NELSON: We all have hidden desires, Peggy. Even a girl like you.

Nelson takes off her hat. She has greased back hair. She gives Peggy a saucy look. Peggy gasps.

118

PEGGY: Oh my God. Maisie!

Nelson lets out a cackle of a laugh like a banshee.

NELSON: I am who you want me to be.

PEGGY: Shut up! You're playing mind games.

NELSON: Isn't that your arena?

PEGGY: I'm not listening to you anymore. You're a liar and a con-merchant.

NELSON: No, you're the liar.

PEGGY: Shut up!

NELSON: No, Peggy. It's showdown time. You lie to people and you keep the truth from them, for your own selfish reasons. Admit it, there's a part of you that is selfish and destructive.

PEGGY: That's not true.

NELSON: It's time to face up to your crimes, Peggy. Anne killed herself because of you.

PEGGY: Shut your mouth!

NELSON: You let her fall in love with her own half-brother. Isn't that true?

Peggy is shocked.

PEGGY: No.

NELSON: Isn't it true?

PEGGY: I tried to stop it.

NELSON: You withheld the truth from her until it was too late.

PEGGY: She was young. I didn't think it would go that far. I thought it would be over within a few weeks.

NELSON: You should have told her sooner. There was plenty of time.

PEGGY: It was difficult.

NELSON: Why was it so difficult to tell Anne that Jim Robinson was her father?

PEGGY: The timing was never right.

NELSON: Another lie.

PEGGY: She loved Willy. I didn't want to break her heart.

NELSON: Another lie, Peggy.

PEGGY: It's the truth!

NELSON: You were protecting yourself.

Peggy shakes her head.

NELSON: You were afraid that if Willy found out about Jim Robinson, you'd lose him for good.

PEGGY: No. I didn't want to hurt him.

NELSON: You held the truth from Anne right to the last possible moment because you didn't want Willy to find out. Isn't that right?

PEGGY: Maybe... I don't know.

NELSON: Aren't you still lying to Willy? You had your chance to tell him the truth and you still lied. Why?

PEGGY: I'm not sure.

NELSON: You're lying.

PEGGY: I don't know.

NELSON: You do.

PEGGY: I was scared.

NELSON: Scared of what?

PEGGY: I don't know.

NELSON: You do.

PEGGY: I don't!

NELSON: SCARED OF WHAT?

PEGGY: Of being on my own! I didn't want to be alone.

Peggy breaks down.

NELSON: But you're alone now, Peggy. Anne is dead, Willy is gone, and you're about to lose Kyle as well. This is where your lies and your bullying have brought you to. An empty house full of bitterness and regret. Can't you see that? Can't you accept that you're to blame?

Peggy nods and starts to cry.

PEGGY: I killed my little girl. I killed her.

Nelson puts her arms around her.

NELSON: That's it, Peggy. That's it. Let it all go. Open the doors of your house and let love seep into every doorframe, every floorboard, every rafter.

Nelson holds Peggy in her arms and rocks her until she falls asleep. When she is asleep, Nelson lies her down on the settee and then exits.

Fourteen

The sun comes up. Birds start singing. Peggy awakens. She walks over to Kyle's bedroom. She's about to speak, but changes her mind and goes into the kitchen. Kyle awakens. He senses things have changed and goes quickly to the door. Peggy enters from the kitchen with two mugs of tea. She walks over to the bedroom door and puts her ear to it. Neither of them realise the other is listening. Finally, Peggy speaks.

PEGGY: Kyle? Kyle?

KYLE: What?

Pause.

PEGGY: Can you see the sun? It's shining. Spring's here.

KYLE: Have you been drinking again?

PEGGY: I've made you a cup of tea.

KYLE: And you expect me to come out and get it?

PEGGY: Yes, I want you to come out and have a cup of tea with me.

KYLE: With you?

PEGGY: Yes, with me.

KYLE: Why should I?

PEGGY: So we can talk.

123

KYLE: We can talk here.

PEGGY: Look, I want you to stay.

Kyle is silent.

PEGGY: Did you hear me? You can stay in the house.

KYLE: How do I know you're not trying to trick me?

PEGGY: You don't, but there's only one way to find out.

Silence.

KYLE: Okay, but stand well clear of the door. (*Peggy moves backwards from the door.*) Are you moving back?

PEGGY: Yes, I'm moving back.

Kyle opens the bedroom door, but stays in the bedroom. Peggy looks past him into the room.

PEGGY: Did you have to make such a mess?

KYLE: Don't start.

PEGGY: But look at the state of it.

KYLE: When you've got nothing to put in your belly, cleanliness is the last thing on your mind.

PEGGY: There's no excuse for untidiness.

KYLE: Do you want me to come out of this room
                 or not?

PEGGY: Okay, I'm sorry. Here.

She holds out the mug of tea. He doesn't move.

PEGGY: Are you going to take it or do you want me
                 to drink it for you as well?

KYLE: Put it on the table and sit down over
                 there.

He points to the armchair.

PEGGY: Christ, it's like an episode of the Bill.

KYLE: Just do it.

PEGGY: Okay, okay.

*Peggy sits. Kyle grabs his bedside lamp for protection. He holds
it out in front of him as he moves to the settee. He sits down,
never taking his eyes of Peggy.*

PEGGY: Do you know how stupid you look?

KYLE: Never mind how I look. Just talk.

PEGGY: What do you want me to say?

KYLE: What do you want to say?

Pause.

125

PEGGY: It's not easy, you know.

KYLE: Don't worry, I'm not going anywhere.

Silence.

PEGGY: Did you know that when you were born, I suffered that Post Natal depression thing? I couldn't bear it when they put you up to my face. Skinny, slimy, little thing with long legs and arms like a spider. I told the nurse I felt sick so she'd take you away. For the first few months I couldn't stand the sight of you. I used to get Anne to dress and feed you. She loved it. Treated you like a doll.

KYLE: Is this meant to make me feel better?

PEGGY: I don't know why it happened with you. I think it was because I had you so late. You made me feel... embarrassed.

KYLE: So I'm to blame for being born now.

PEGGY: I didn't say that. Just let me finish, will you? (*Pause.*)

There was one day when everything changed. I can still see it as if it was yesterday. It was a clear, winter's day. You must have been about four months old. I was in the kitchen, cleaning as usual, and

126

you were lying in your basket in the living room. No one else was in. Nelson Eddy and Jeanette MacDonald were playing on the turntable. Out of the blue I heard this strange, little, high-pitched sound. At first I thought it was a bird outside, but then I realised it was coming from the living room. I ran in and there you were, in your basket - and I swear to God you were singing along to Nelson and Jeanette. You looked so beautiful. I lifted you up into my arms and held you tight. From that moment on I grew to love you more than anything... anyone.

KYLE: So what happened?

PEGGY: I still love you.

Pause.

KYLE: You've had a funny way of showing it.

PEGGY: I know, but I want to change all that.

KYLE: Even though I'm gay.

PEGGY: Yes.

KYLE: What about Donal? Donal and me.

PEGGY: Well... Donal seems like a nice boy...

KYLE: And?

PEGGY: And I'm sure he'll make a great son-in-law…

KYLE: Very fuckin' funny.

PEGGY: What do you want me to say?

KYLE: That you're okay about it. That you'll welcome him into the house. That you'll accept we're a couple.

PEGGY: You don't want much, do you?

KYLE: I didn't starve myself for nothing.

PEGGY: I can't give any promises but I'm going to try. Is that okay?

KYLE: I suppose it'll have to be.

Peggy stands.

PEGGY: Good. Now how about a big fry?

Peggy walks towards the kitchen.

KYLE: Ma?

Peggy stops and turns.

PEGGY: Do you want two fried eggs?

KYLE: Donal's found a flat in the Holy Lands. I'm gonna move in with him – if he'll still have me.

PEGGY: Oh…

Peggy sits down again.

KYLE: I'm not doing it to punish you. I swear.

PEGGY: So all this...

KYLE: It's just... time. I'm twenty two. I can't stay here forever.

Peggy nods, unable to speak. Kyle goes to her and takes her hand.

KYLE: Are you okay?

PEGGY: I'm fine. I'm fine.

KYLE: Are you sure?

Pause.

PEGGY: How about a song?

KYLE: What?

PEGGY: A song. Come on. Just one song. The one I used to sing to you when you were a wean.

KYLE: Fuck off, Ma!

Peggy starts to sing Smilin' Through. Kyle is embarrassed at first, but joins in. He gets the words wrong and sings Shinin' Through.

PEGGY: Smilin' Through, Smilin' Through! Not fuckin' Shinin' Through!

The End.

Still Ill

by Billy Cowan

Still Ill was produced by Truant Company in association with the Oldham Coliseum and with the generous support of Arts Council England and The National Lottery.It was first performed at The Lowry Studio, Salford on 14th November 2014 with the following cast:

TOMMY MILLS	Neal McWilliams
GARY MCDAID	Sean Croke
ELAINE MILLS	Alison Darling
DAVE MILLS	Ian Curley

Director	Joyce Branagh
Designer	Alison Heffernan
Lighting designer	Mark Alexander
Sound	Jamie Summers

Truant would like to thank the following people and organisations who have helped in the journey towards production:

Arts Council England; Kevin Shaw, Artistic Director at Oldham Coliseum; 24:7 Theatre Festival; Chris Bridgman; Punam Ramchurn, Artistic Director of Rochdale Literature and Ideas Festival; Gary Everett, Artistic Director of Homotopia; Simon Bent and Manchester Salon; Edge Hill University.

Characters:

Tommy Mills   39 years old

Elaine Mills   39 years old

Dave Mills   45 years old

Gary McDaid   39 years old

A member of a paramilitaryorganisation

The play takes place in 2008, ten years after the signing of the Good Friday Agreement, in a small town on the Ards Peninsula, County Down, Northern Ireland. There are three locations: The Naughty But Nice Adult Shop; Elaine and Dave's dining room/kitchen; an old air-raid shelter on the banks of Strangford Lough.

/ indicates when a line of dialogue is interrupted by the following line.

The member of the paramilitary organisation can be played by the actor playing Dave.

All rights to perform There is a Light that Never Goes Out by Steven Morrissey and Johnny Marr must be obtained from the relevant copyright sources.

133

ACT ONE

Scene 1

The sex shop. Elaine is singing to herself and hanging some sexy underwear up. Dave enters.

DAVE: Here.

He hands her a pregnancy test kit.

ELAINE: It's too early to tell.

DAVE: Do it anyway.

ELAINE: No. It'll be a waste. I'll do it at the weekend.

DAVE: Do it now. Come on.

ELAINE: I won't be pregnant, honey. I'm a woman, I know these things.

DAVE: Do it.

ELAINE: Don't you think there's other more important things you should be thinkin' about right now?

DAVE: Fuck them.

ELAINE: No, Dave. They'll fuck you if you don't get it sorted out.

DAVE: Fancy another try, right here in the shop?

ELAINE: Have you taken anything? Have you?

DAVE:	I've told you, I'm not fuckin' usin'. Now do you want a shag or not?
ELAINE:	Thought you were paintin' that wall for me this mornin'?
DAVE:	For fuck sake, that bloody house. Is that all you think about?
ELAINE:	I want it lukin nice, Dave.
DAVE:	Alright, I'm goin'. It's obvious you don't want me here. I'll see you tonight.

He exits. Elaine throws the pregnancy test in the binand goes back to work. The doorbell rings and Tommy enters wheeling a suitcase.

ELAINE:	Tommy!
TOMMY:	How are you, you old tart?
ELAINE:	Come here, you big fuckin' poof.

They hug each other.

	I can't believe yer here. Let me luk at you. You haven't changed a bit, so you haven't. Yer still the best lukin man in the County a Down.
TOMMY:	And you're still the best lookin' slapper.
ELAINE:	Fuck off, you cheeky bastard.

They hug again.

135

TOMMY:	It's good to see you.
ELAINE:	Eight years is a long time.
TOMMY:	That's not my fault, Elaine.

Pause.

ELAINE:	Look, let's have a cupatay an' a right oul natter. I'll put up the closed sign.
TOMMY:	I've got to check in by two.
ELAINE:	What do you mean? Aren't you stayin' with us?
TOMMY:	I'd rather kip down in a pile of cow shite than spend one night under the same roof as that bastard. (*Pause.*) Sorry.
ELAINE:	It doesn't bother me what you say, coz yer right -he is a bastard.

She goes into a back room to make the tea. Tommy looks around at all the sex toys.

TOMMY:	I'm staying at The Strangford. Sixty quid a night for a dump like that, can you believe it? I suppose now there's peace they think they can charge what they want.
ELAINE:	It's been all done up since you were here. Thinks it's The Europa now. They do good grub but. I usually go down with Dave for their Sunday Roast.

136

TOMMY: Didn't this place used to be the old police station?

ELAINE: Yeah. Ironic, isn't it?

TOMMY: I can't believe the changes.

ELAINE: I know. Everything's bein' turned into fancy apartments or shops. Even Stormont.

TOMMY: Come off it.

ELAINE: Oh yeah, half a million each they're gonna cost. Des-res for the politically minded.

TOMMY: Fuck off!

ELAINE: Of course not, you soft shite.

Tommy picks up a dildo.

TOMMY: It's hard to believe the oul town has a sex shop.

ELAINE: We refer to it as the Adult Learning Centre, if you don't mind.

Tommy laughs.

TOMMY: What made you open up a sex shop anyway?

ELAINE: It was Dave's idea.

TOMMY:	I might have known. Wasn't a newsagents or a clothes shop good enough for Mr Big Time Davy Mills?
ELAINE:	You know what he's like.
TOMMY:	Yeah. A pathetic, attention-seeking little boy.
ELAINE:	What?
TOMMY:	(*Quickly*) How did you get it past the Ulster Says No brigade?

Elaine sticks her head out.

ELAINE:	We give them free wank mags.
TOMMY:	Come off it.
ELAINE:	Oh, a lot has changed since you were here Mister. We're now the sex an' drugs capital of the North. We have swinger nights down at The Oul Cross. And you'll love this... there's even a cruising ground for dirty oul queers like yerself.
TOMMY:	Fuck away off.
ELAINE:	There is, I'm tellin' you. It's way down the Shore Road in the bushes beside that oul air-raid shelter. You remember, the one where we used to go campin'.

138

TOMMY: No way. How come the peelers or the para's don't put a stop to it?

ELAINE: Nobody goes down there anymore, so nobody knows about it – except the select few.

TOMMY: And you're one of the select few, are you?

ELAINE: It's amazing what info you pick up workin' in a sex shop.

TOMMY: I might just pop down there later to see if it's true.

ELAINE: You dirty bastard.

She goes into the back room again.

TOMMY: Hey these butt plugs are double the price you pay for them in England.

ELAINE: I know. But we're the only half-decent sex shop for miles, so we can charge what we want.

She comes out with two cups of tea.

Here. Milk an' two sugars, if ma memory serves me well.

TOMMY: Actually I take it black with no sugar now.

ELAINE: Get it down yer throat.

TOMMY: Milk aggravates my Post Nasal Drip Syndrome.

ELAINE: Catch yerself on.

TOMMY: It does, seriously.

ELAINE: Still a hypochrondriac, I see.

TOMMY: It's a real condition.

ELAINE: Well yer not gettin' another one, so you'll have to make do. Now stop complainin' an' tell me what you've been gettin' up to for eight years.

TOMMY: What do you want to know?

ELAINE: Everything, includin' the bits you don't want me to know.

TOMMY: Where do I start?

ELAINE: Tell me about this man of yers - Toby. How big is his cock? An' how long have you been seein' him?

TOMMY: His cock is bigger than what you've ever seen and it's been five years. We even have an allotment.

ELAINE: Five years – his cock must be big.

TOMMY: Piss off. It takes more than a big cock to keep me interested.

ELAINE: I know, I know - you always liked them to have a brain as well.

TOMMY: There's nothing wrong in that. You should try it sometime.

Pause.

ELAINE: So what's this Toby one like then?

TOMMY: Great. He cooks, I clean. He's practical and straightforward, I'm artistic and complicated. We're a perfect match. Couldn't be better.

ELAINE: Civil partnership?

TOMMY: What do you think?

ELAINE: They do it here, you know. At the Town Hall.

TOMMY: The times they are a changin'.

ELAINE: Did you see those two fenian dykes on the news -the ones who did it first?

TOMMY: Yeah. I thought they were brave as fuck - what with all those Presbyterian bastards outside.

ELAINE: They'll be divorced in a couple a months, wait an' see.

Pause.

TOMMY: So how are things with you otherwise?

ELAINE: Oh, the same old.

TOMMY: No weans yet?

ELAINE: Let's not go there.

TOMMY: Don't tell me big boy Dave's got problems down below.

ELAINE: He's lucky to have me, never mind weans.

TOMMY: Oh, I take it all's not well in the House of Love then.

ELAINE: You could say that.

Pause.

TOMMY: Alright, what's up? Tell Tommy. It sounded serious on the phone.

Pause.

ELAINE: He's dealin' again.

TOMMY: What in -stocks and shares?

ELAINE: It's not funny, Tommy. If he doesn't stop, he's a dead man. The Boys are onto him. They came into the shop the other day and put a bullet on the counter. They said if he didn't cease activities immediately and hand over fifteen grand he'd be dead before the week was out.

142

TOMMY: Can't you get the peelers to do something?

ELAINE: Those fuckers were useless before the peace an' they're even more useless now.

TOMMY: What do you expect me to do? I can hardly take on the bully boys myself.

ELAINE: Have a word with Dave. See if you can get him to stop. Nothin' I say works.

TOMMY: And you expect him to listen to me -his queer brother who according to him killed his own Ma.

ELAINE: He didn't mean that. He was upset. People say things they don't mean at funerals.

TOMMY: Does that include you?

ELAINE: I had to take his side, Tommy. He's my husband.

TOMMY: It hurt me.

ELAINE: I know. I'm sorry.

TOMMY: And do you still agree with him?

ELAINE: About the house?

Tommy nods.

No. You were right not to give him anything.

143

TOMMY: But you'd like me to give him fifteen grand now?

ELAINE: I didn't say that, Tommy. I just thought you could persuade him to stop dealin'.

TOMMY: Come off it Elaine. I'm not stupid.

Pause.

ELAINE: Alright, if you've got the money and could loan us it I'd be very happy. But I swear Tommy that's not the reason I got you over. I just want you to talk some sense into him.

TOMMY: Look Elaine, he's got himself into this mess, he can get himself out of it.

ELAINE: They'll kill him, Tommy.

TOMMY: Give me a gun and I'll do it for them.

ELAINE: You don't mean that.

TOMMY: Don't I?

ELAINE: He's all the family you've got.

TOMMY: My family is across the water in Manchester. They're a small group of gay men and women who love and respect me, and yes they mightn't share the same DNA but they're family all the same.

ELAINE: And what am I? Just some stupid cow who happened to marry yer brother - who you lost yer virginity to - who supported you when you first came out and kicked the livin' shit outta anyone who called you a queer bastard?

Pause.

Don't you care what happens to me? Coz it's not just him they'll hurt. At best they'll force me to sell the house and the shop and give them the proceeds. At worst they'll put a bullet through my head as well. You don't know what it's like Tommy. You don't live here anymore. The rats haven't fled the sinkin' ship, they've grown fins an' taken over.

She is upset.

TOMMY: I'm sorry. I'm a selfish twat.

ELAINE: Will you come round tonight? Have a word with him?

Pause.

Come on, please. I'll make supper. How about some stew? You always loved a dish a stew. Bet you haven't had it in a while.

TOMMY: I'm vegetarian now.

145

ELAINE: For fuck sake.

Pause.

               Will you come round?

TOMMY: Put some beans in it instead of meat and I'll think about it.

She playfully hits him. They smile.

Scene 2

Dave sits in the dining-room area of the kitchen drinking a can of Harp. The room is in the process of being redecorated, so the walls are stripped and things look messy. Elaine and Tommy enter, drinking from wine glasses.

TOMMY: It's a great house. You've got it looking lovely, Elaine. Do you fancy coming over and doing mine? Toby and I are working all the time so nothing gets done. The bedroom walls haven't seen a lick of paint since they were replastered six months ago. It's a tip. Did you decorate yourselves or did you get someone in?

ELAINE: Dave did most of it himself. Didn't you, Dave?

Dave doesn't respond.

It's taken a while – what with the shop an' all, but we're gettin' there. Only this room to do now.

TOMMY: And what's the colour scheme in here going to be?

ELAINE: Green.

DAVE: Like fuck.

ELAINE: Oh it can speak then.

147

TOMMY:	Alright, Dave.
DAVE:	So what brings you back hame? Missing yer big brother were you?
TOMMY:	Oh aye, couldn't live without you.
DAVE:	Well somethin' must have brung you back.

Tommy doesn't know what to say.

ELAINE:	I asked him to, Dave. Alright? I thought it was about time youse two made it up.
DAVE:	That's awfully considerate of you, darlin'. But in future can you let me make my own fuckin' decisions.
ELAINE:	Don't start.
TOMMY:	If you don't want me to be here Dave, just say the word and I'll go. It's no skin off my teeth.
DAVE:	Did I say I wanted you to go?
TOMMY:	No, but I don't see you laying out the red carpet.
DAVE:	If my darlin' wife had given me more notice I might have put out the flags an' the buntin'. Would that have pleased you?

Pause.

ELAINE: Here, guess who I bumped into the other day? Big Pamela Davidson. You remember Pamela, don't you Dave? She used to run about with Tommy an' me -had orange hair like Annie Lennox. Well wait till you hear this - she's had a black wean.

DAVE: Christ, what's this country comin' to?

ELAINE: Don't be like that, Dave. The wean was beautiful.

DAVE: Yeah, but look at what it'll turn into.

ELAINE: Don't be so fuckin' racist, you. Anyway, a year ago she met this fella from Kenya on the internet, fell in love with him...

DAVE: Stupid bitch.

ELAINE: ...and went over to Africa to marry him.

TOMMY: Only Big Pamela Davidson could do something like that.

ELAINE: I know. Anyway, turns out he only wanted her for a passport. So when he got over here, he fucked off with a skinny slapper from Bangor an' left her houlin' the wean in a flea-ridden bedsit on Dufferin Avenue. She's got no money, God love her, and she looks like shit. She says Benjie, that's the wean, keeps her up all night gurnin'.

149

DAVE: I'll be fuckin' gurnin' if you don't hurry up an' dish out that stew.

ELAINE: Keep yer knickers on. I'll get it now.

Elaine goes into the kitchen area. Silence.

TOMMY: Looks like you're doing well for yourself - what with the shop and all.

DAVE: Can't complain. What about you?

TOMMY: Yeah, I'm doing okay. Head Graphic Designer for a multimedia company.

DAVE: What the fuck's a multimedia company?

TOMMY: They design and construct intranet systems for big businesses - that type of thing.

DAVE: You mean websites?

TOMMY: Yeah, kind of.

DAVE: Then why didn't you say that?

ELAINE: Cut it out, Dave.

TOMMY: It's okay, Elaine.

DAVE: And how much does this multimedia company pay you?

ELAINE: Dave, for fuck sake.

TOMMY: Thirty-five grand a year. Do you wanna see a payslip?

ELAINE: Jesus, that's amazing Tommy.

DAVE: Ma always said if you fell out off a boat you'd come up with a salmon in yer pocket.

TOMMY: It's got nothing to do with luck. I work hard for that money.

DAVE: That makes a change.

TOMMY: What's that supposed to mean?

DAVE: Well, you haven't worked hard for every penny you received. Have you?

ELAINE: Don't listen to him, Tommy.

TOMMY: Look Dave, I've come over here as a favour to Elaine to help you get sorted out.So let's not get sucked into arguments about the past that no-one can win. Let's just be civil to each other for once.

DAVE: What do you mean 'to help me get sorted out'? (*To Elaine*) Have you been spillin' yer guts bitch?

ELAINE: I had to speak to someone.

DAVE: I knew it. You couldn't houl in yer own piss if you tried.

ELAINE: I'm fuckin' scared that's why.

TOMMY: Why are you dealing anyway? Doesn't the shop bring in enough?

DAVE: Let's get this straight once an'for all – I'm not fuckin' dealin'. I sell to a few pals just to get enough to cover the mortgage and the lease and that's it. And any how it's got nothin' to do with you.

TOMMY: When the Boys hand you a bullet with your name engraved on it, it must be more serious than selling to your mates.

DAVE: They're a pack a small time hoodlums who don't know shit. They don't scare me.

TOMMY: Small time hoodlums with guns, Dave. So wise up and cut it out. Don't be a selfish twat all your life. Think about Elaine.

DAVE: Don't fuckin' dare come into my house an' call me a selfish twat.

TOMMY: Sorry. I didn't mean it.

DAVE: If anyone's a selfish twat it's you.

ELAINE: Dave honey, relax.

DAVE: Yer the cunt who refused to come back ha me to see yer own Ma even though you knew she was on her last breath.

TOMMY: The last time I saw her she told me, in no uncertain terms, to piss off back to England - that she didn't want to see my queer face again.

DAVE: Ach you poor thing. So you ran back to England with yer tail between yer legs, gurnin' like a spoilt brat. Ma's wee son goin' into a huff like he always did.

TOMMY: I wanted to come back, but it was difficult. I didn't want to look like a hypocrite.

DAVE: You didn't worry about lukin like a hypocrite when you took her house and her money.

TOMMY: Here we go.

DAVE: Well did you?

TOMMY: What did you expect me to do? Donate it to the billy boy's prisoner's fund or give it to you so you could sniff it up your fuckin' nose.

Dave jumps up to hit him. Elaine intercepts him.

ELAINE: Dave! Leave it! Come on, sit down.

He reluctantly sits back down.

TOMMY: Look, Elaine. I'm sorry. I tried, but I'll see you around.

153

ELAINE: Tommy, don't be daft.

He exits.

Are you just gonna sit there?

Dave doesn't move. Elaine runs after Tommy.

Tommy, wait!

Dave takes a wrap of coke out of his pocket and does a line.

Scene 3

Night. The bushes beside the Air-Raid shelter which is surrounded by a wire fence with warning signs - Keep Out, Demolition site etc. Tommy walks up and down talking on his mobile.

TOMMY: I know, but what can I do? I've told her she can come back with me if she wants, but... well, she loves him. Yeah. And anyway she hates the English. She said she'd rather have a bullet through her head than spend the rest of her life across the pond with the roundheads. (*He laughs*) I know, she's a tough bitch. You'd like her. Anyway, I better go. I'm gonna catch a bite to eat in the hotel bar then go to bed. (*Pause*) Yeah. Okay. Love ya and see ya tomorrow.

He hangs up. After a few seconds a man appears in the bushes. He steps out and they stare at each other for a few seconds. The man lights a cigarette. Tommy recognises him.

TOMMY: Gary? Gary McDaid?

Gary dives into the bushes.

Gary! It's Tommy. Tommy Mills. Get your arse back here now.

Gary eventually appears.

GARY:	Well, well, well. If it isn't the jumped up pantry boy.
TOMMY:	And the boy with the thorn in his side.
GARY:	Millsey, you wee fruit. It's great to see you. What are you doin' here?
TOMMY:	What are *you* doin' here?
GARY:	Oh I'm just out for a walk - gettin' the oul head shired, you know.
TOMMY:	A walk?
GARY:	Yeah, a walk.
TOMMY:	Down here, in the middle of nowhere?
GARY:	Yeah, have you got a problem with that?

Tommy laughs.

TOMMY:	No, not at all.
GARY:	Good.
TOMMY:	So when did this... passion for walking start?
GARY:	Fuck away off, Millsey.
TOMMY:	Well come off it, Gaz. A walk! You could have come up with something a bit more original than that.

GARY: Don't you crack onto anyone you saw me here, Millsey. D'you hear? I mean it.

TOMMY: Don't worry your secret is safe with me.

GARY: It fuckin' better be.

TOMMY: Drop the hard man act, Gaz. It doesn't cut the mustard. I'm the one you used to snog the face off when you were a spotty teenager pissed outta your head on red witches, remember?

GARY: I only snogged you cuz you were better lukin than all the millies that lived round here. Didn't mean I wanted to get my cock up yer arse.

TOMMY: Maybe you secretly wanted mine up yours.

GARY: Aye, that'id be right.

Pause.

TOMMY: The last time I saw you was just after my twentieth birthday.

GARY: So it was. Just before you pissed off to uni-fuckin-varsity with all yer posh friends.

TOMMY: That's almost twenty years ago. Can you believe it?

GARY: Hey, do you remember this?

157

He sings the chorus from There Is A Light That Never Goes Out by The Smiths. Tommy joins him in the last line. They laugh.

Those were the days.

TOMMY: Yeah. The hunger strikes. The bombings. The riots. The unemployment. Great stuff.

GARY: If some bastard built a time machine, I'd go back in an instant.

Pause.

TOMMY: So what are you up to, besides coming down here to get yer knob sucked?

GARY: Hey, I'm a married man. Watch what yer sayin'.

TOMMY: Married?

GARY: Yep, with three wee girls. Here.

He takes a photo out of his wallet and shows Tommy.

TOMMY: They're pretty. Must take after their Ma.

GARY: Cunt.

They smile.

So what brings you back over hame?

TOMMY: Don't ask.

GARY: Dave?

TOMMY: What makes you say that?

GARY: He's yer brother, isn't he?

TOMMY: Right.

GARY: Have you seen Elaine yet?

TOMMY: Yeah. She's still the same.

GARY: We used to have some crackin' times together, didn't we?

TOMMY: Aye... some.

GARY: Don't be a miserable bastard... we had a ball.

TOMMY: Like the time you almost got us shot driving through that checkpoint on the Ormeau Road after The Smiths gig at the Ulster Hall.

GARY: My foot slipped on the accelerator.

TOMMY: You did it on purpose.

Gary laughs.

GARY: Elaine pissed her knickers when she saw those squaddies surroundin' the car and pointin' their rifles.

TOMMY: You were a mad fucker.

Gary laughs.

GARY:	So how long are you over for?
TOMMY:	I'm heading back tomorrow.
GARY:	Oh.

Pause.

TOMMY:	Don't tell me you're disappointed?
GARY:	Na, I was just wondering if you'd give us a wank.

Gary smiles playfully.

TOMMY:	I knew it, you bastard. Elaine always said there was something funny about you.
GARY:	I'm straight. I only do this for a bit a fun.
TOMMY:	That's what they all say.

Pause.

GARY:	So how about it?
TOMMY:	No way.
GARY:	Come on, live a bit Millsey.
TOMMY:	Twenty years ago I would have jumped at the chance.
GARY:	And twenty years ago I would have smacked yer head in if you'd tried.

He smiles.

TOMMY: You knew I was mad about you then, didn't you?

GARY: Don't know what yer talkin' about.

TOMMY: Yes you do.

GARY: I'm telling you, I don't.

TOMMY: Well, I was. That's why I treated all your girlfriends like shit. And that's why I left the fuckin' country. I was so in love with you, it was making me sick. I had to get away or I would have topped myself.

GARY: That's understandable – I was a handsome devil.

TOMMY: You're an arrogant twat. I don't know what I ever saw in you.

Gary laughs.

GARY: Do you fancy makin' up for lost time then?

TOMMY: No way.

GARY: Why not? Yer leavin' tomorrow.

TOMMY: As much as I'd like to... no.

GARY: Are you afraid you might not be able to handle the big yin?

He playfully grabs himself between the legs.

161

TOMMY: I can handle that, Gaz. It's what comes with it that scares me. I'll see you around.

He goes to leave.

GARY: Millsey! Why don't you stay a few more days? Come on. Let's have a laugh. It'll be like oul times. What do you say?

Tommy hesitates and then exits. Gary shouts the chorus from 'There Is A Light That Never Goes Out.'

Scene 4

Next day. The Sex Shop. Tommy enters.

TOMMY: (*Putting on a strong accent*) Excuse me luv, you haven't got a big black dildo I could shove up my ass an' ride the houl way to Newry an' back?

ELAINE: Tommy! Thought you were catchin' a plane back to England.

TOMMY: I've had second thoughts. I've decided to give that bastard another chance. God knows why.

ELAINE: I knew you wouldn't let me down.

TOMMY: I'm a soft shite me, that's my trouble.

ELAINE: You know he was devastated last night when you left.

TOMMY: Clear off, Elaine. Who are you trying to kid?

ELAINE: He was. I could tell.

TOMMY: Yeah well, he should learn to keep his big mouth shut then.

ELAINE: He needs to get it off his chest, Tommy, and yer gonna have to accept that. I know he's a bad-tempered fucker, but yer gonna have to try and talk to him.

163

TOMMY: I'm not sure he's interested in talkin'. As far as he's concerned, he's right and I'm wrong and that's all there is to it. I mean, I know what I did was shit - that I should have swallowed my pride and come over to see her. Christ, there isn't a day goes bywhen I don't beat myself up about it. But I spent my whole life letting her get away with... things, you know. I just felt I had to make a stand. All I wanted was for her to call *me* for once - for her to say sorry to *me* for once. Was that so fuckin' terrible?

ELAINE: Don't explain it to me, Tommy. I understand. It's not me you need to convince. It's him.

TOMMY: I know... and I'm going to.

ELAINE: Good, coz if you can get this sorted out, he might listen to you about the drugs.

TOMMY: I wouldn't hold your breath.

ELAINE: I'm so used to houlin' my breath, I could be a bloody deep sea diver.

Tommy smiles.

TOMMY: Where is he now? Is he at home?

ELAINE: He should be.

TOMMY: Right, no time like the present.

ELAINE: Do you want me to come with you?

TOMMY: No. We'll fight it out together like we always do.

ELAINE: Thanks, Tommy.

TOMMY: No problem.

He goes to leave.

TOMMY: By the way, I've got a nice bit of juicy gossip for you later on.

ELAINE: What is it?

TOMMY: See ya.

He exits with a wave.

Scene 5

Later. Dave and Elaine's house. Dave is sitting at the table reading The Sun. Tommy enters from the kitchen door.

DAVE: If yer lukin for Elaine, she's at the shop.

TOMMY: It's you I want to see. I want us to talk.

DAVE: Talk? Must be serious. Do you mind if I grab a beer first?

He fetches a beer from the fridge.

Do you want one?

TOMMY: No, thanks.

DAVE: Oh aye, I forgot. Beer goes for yer stomach.

TOMMY: I don't want us to fight, Dave.

DAVE: Why should now be any different?

TOMMY: Because Ma's dead and there's only us two left.

DAVE: And that's meant to make us the best a pals, is it?

TOMMY: I want us to get along.

DAVE: Alright. Let's get along. I'll say somethin' meaningless about the weather and you can agree.

TOMMY: For fuck sake, Dave.

DAVE: What's the matter? Aren't I makin' this easy enough for you?

TOMMY: If you give me a chance, I wanna apologise.

DAVE: Apologise? This should be good.

TOMMY: I mean it. I'm sorry for not coming back home before she died. I shouldn't have let you go through all that on your own. I was a selfish twat and there's no excuse.

DAVE: This beer tastes good.

TOMMY: I'm trying my best here.

DAVE: Well, what do you expect me to say? That all's forgiven – that I understand – that I'd have done the same if I'd been in yer shoes?

TOMMY: I just want you to except my apology and agree to move on. (*Pause.*) And let me try to make amends.

DAVE: And how are you goin' to do that?

TOMMY: I thought I could start by paying off the Boys for you. (*Dave laughs.*) Fifteen grand. That's not to be laughed at.

DAVE: Yer so fuckin' kind.

TOMMY: I'm willing to do that for you, Dave.

167

DAVE:	For yerself, you mean - to ease yer fuckin' conscience.
TOMMY:	Alright, if that's what you want to think, fine. But it's still fifteen grand and that's a helluva lot of money.
DAVE:	And what do you expect me to do for this fifteen grand?
TOMMY:	I'd hope you'd give up the dealin'.
DAVE:	I'll give up the dealin' when you cough up half a what you got for Ma's house. (*Pause.*) Yes, Tommy. If you really want to make amends you'll give me half of what you got for the house.
TOMMY:	I haven't got it. It all went into the house in Manchester.
DAVE:	Re-mortgage.

Pause.

TOMMY:	No.
DAVE:	It's rightfully mine.
TOMMY:	It's not.
DAVE:	The house should have been divided equally.
TOMMY:	Ma obviously didn't want that.

DAVE: She didn't have the sense to know what she wanted.

TOMMY: She had the sense to know you'd squander anything she left behind.

DAVE: The money will go into the shop.

TOMMY: You've got to give The Boys fifteen grand, Dave – that's fifteen grand you've already wasted. How much more money do you want to throw away?

DAVE: The money is for the shop. It won't be wasted.

TOMMY: I don't believe you.

DAVE: I don't care what you fuckin' believe – that money is owed to me and I want it back.

TOMMY: For fuck sake, grow up! I owe you nothing. The world owes you nothing. Stop thinking you're hard done by. It's pathetic. It makes me sick to the stomach and it made Ma sick to the stomach. No wonder she left you fuck all.

Dave jumps up and grabs Tommy.

DAVE: Shut yer fuckin' mouth! Shut yer fuckin' queer mouth!

They struggle.

169

TOMMY: Let go! Let me fuckin' go!

Dave eventually lets him go.

TOMMY: I don't know what more I can do.

DAVE: You can give me the money.

TOMMY: She wanted me to have it. I have to respect that.

DAVE: Like you respected her when she wanted you to come back?

TOMMY: Can't you see that's why I have to keep the money? I owe her that.

DAVE: Fuck off, Tommy. You make me sick.

Pause.

TOMMY: Fifteen grand is a lot of money, Dave. I'd think about it if I were you.

Tommy exits.

Scene 6

Night. The cruising ground. Tommy paces up and down in front of the air-raid shelter. He's still upset by the fight with Dave. Gary appears.

GARY: I had a feelin' you'd stay.

Tommy kisses him. Gary pushes him off. They look at each other for a moment and then Tommy desperately kisses him again. They start to make passionate, almost violent, love.

Scene 7

Next day at the Shop. Elaine is rearranging some clothes on a rail. Tommy enters.

ELAINE: Where have you been? I was tryin' to reach you all night.

TOMMY: I was catching up with some mates.

ELAINE: Dave told me you fought again. I'm sorry, Tommy. I shouldn't have got you involved.

TOMMY: He wants me to re-mortgage my house.

ELAINE: What?

TOMMY: To give him half of what Ma left.

ELAINE: I'll fuckin' kill him when I see him.

Pause.

TOMMY: You think I should, don't you?

ELAINE: No, Tommy. Eight years ago, I did. But not now. Yer ma left the house to you and I can see why.

TOMMY: Maybe I should just do it. I've never felt comfortable about taking it.

ELAINE: Yer not givin' him a penny.

TOMMY: But he was there for her. Where the fuck was I?

ELAINE: He was there for her when she was dyin' but he wasn't there for her when she was living. You were.

Pause.

TOMMY: You may be right.

ELAINE: I know I'm right.

TOMMY: Still, I think I should give you the fifteen grand to pay off the Boys.

ELAINE: No, Tommy. I've thought it over. I'm gonna sell the business.

TOMMY: I don't want you to do that. I can see how much it means to you.

ELAINE: If it gets the Boys off our backs I don't mind.

TOMMY: I want to give you the fifteen grand, Elaine.

ELAINE: No.

TOMMY: I'm giving you the money and that's the end of it.

ELAINE: I don't want it.

TOMMY: You're bloody well going to take it.

ELAINE: No. I'm selling the shop. I'll be glad to get shot of it.

TOMMY: Elaine, I'm not taking no for an answer. I'm giving you the money. Now shut your cake-hole before I change my mind.

Pause.

ELAINE: Alright, Tommy. But only if it's a loan.

TOMMY: Look, just send me a fresh supply of wank mags every now and again and I'll be happy.

ELAINE: Are you sure?

TOMMY: Yes, for God's sake.

ELAINE: Thanks. You've saved his life.

TOMMY: Do you think he'll stop?

ELAINE: If he doesn't I'll put a bullet through his head myself, never mind Gary fuckin' McDaid.

TOMMY: Gary McDaid?

ELAINE: Yeah. He's one a the Boys. (*Pause.*) What's the matter?

TOMMY: Are you sure? The Gary McDaid I know would never get involved with paramilitaries.

ELAINE: Take my word for it – he has. The whole town pays him protection money.

174

TOMMY: But he used to hate all that macho bullshit as much as we did.

ELAINE: People change, Tommy.

Pause.

Oh no. You've seen him, haven't you? You need to take my word for it Tommy, he's trouble. So keep well away. I know how you felt about him when we were younger but that was a long time ago. He's no longer the lovable rogue we used to know.

TOMMY: I'm going to speak to him.

ELAINE: Don't be fuckin' stupid. Tommy …

He exits.

Scene 8

Night. The cruising ground. Gary sits beside the air-raid shelter. Tommy arrives.

GARY: Millsey, over here. Jump over.

Tommy climbs over the wire fence and goes to him.

Back so soon. I'm hard to resist.

TOMMY: Yes, I've been hearing how hard it is for people to say no to you.

GARY: What's that supposed to mean?

TOMMY: Can't you work it out?

GARY: Fuck off, Millsey. Here, look what I've brung us.

He takes out a bottle of Ye Olde English Cider from a plastic bag.

TOMMY: We're turning forty this year. Not seventeen.

GARY: Lighten up, for fuck sake. Years with all those English bastards has done nothin' for yer sense a humour.

TOMMY: And what has years of living here done to you, Gaz? Tell me that.

GARY: It's made me realise you need to grab the good times while you can. Now drink up.

Tommy refuses to take the bottle.

> For fuck sake, I'll have it myself then.

He drinks from the bottle.

TOMMY: When, Gaz?

GARY: When what?

TOMMY: When did you become like all the rest.

GARY: You've only been here five minutes an' already yer doin' my head in. Now if yer not gonna have a drink with me, you can clear off.

TOMMY: So it's true.

GARY: So what's fuckin' true?

TOMMY: That you're one of the big men who knock on people's doors in the middle of the night with a baseball bat or a semi-automatic.

GARY: Keep yer voice down.

TOMMY: Why? Are you ashamed? Don't you want the men who suck yer cock to know that you're a piece of scum?

GARY: You should look closer to hame, Millsey, if you wanna know what scum is.

TOMMY: Dave may be a druggie but he's no killer.

177

GARY:	He would sell crack to an eight year old if he thought the wean had enough money in his piggy bank to pay for it.
TOMMY:	And you're a hundred per cent sure of that, are you?
GARY:	We've been watchin' him.
TOMMY:	And who appointed you guardian of the people?
GARY:	The people.
TOMMY:	Fuck off.
GARY:	We make the town a safe place to live in. The people want us.
TOMMY:	You know that's not true.
GARY:	Sure what would you know, Millsey. You don't live here anymore. You don't even sound like yer from here - what with yer English fuckin' tongue. Yer an outsider, for God's sake.
TOMMY:	If being an Ulsterman means being like you, then I'm glad I'm an outsider.
GARY:	Ach, fuck away off.

Pause.

TOMMY: Just tell me why, Gaz. You were different to the others. You had a brain in your head. You liked The Smiths for God's sake. What happened? And don't tell me you didn't have a choice because that's too easy. There's always a bloody choice.

GARY: Yer right, Millsey. I could have told them to fuck off when they put a gun to the back a my knees. I could have chosen to spend the rest a my life in a wheelchair – who knows I might even have entered the spastic Olympics and won a gold fuckin' medal. But you know what? It was easier to say yes. And do you want to know something else? I didn't mind because I was growin' so fuckin' angry at seein' all the people around me get killed. That's why I joined. I could have left the country like you – run away to the bright lights and the big cities where Kick the Pope bands and car bombs were things you only read about in papers, but I chose to stay and fight because I cared about the people around me.

TOMMY: And what's your excuse now? Now that the killings have stopped? Now that the war is over?

GARY: Alright, I'll tell you. Sheer fuckin' fear.
                 Fear a not knowin' what else to do - fear a
                 bein' bumped off if I ask to get out - fear a
                 havin' to grow up. You name it and I'm
                 fuckin' feared of it.

*Tommy is knocked back by Gary's candour. He doesn't know
what to say. Finally...*

TOMMY: Is that why you ran off the other night after
                 / we'd...

GARY: I've never... with a man I've known before.
                 I didn't know what to say.

Pause.

TOMMY: You should have told me about the para's.

*Gary sits down and takes another drink from the bottle of cider.
He offers it to Tommy. Tommy remains standing.*

GARY: Do you remember the night we camped out
                 in there? Me, you, and Elaine, and some
                 other wee millie who I can't remember now.

TOMMY: Big Pamela Davidson.

GARY: What?

TOMMY: It was big Pamela Davidson.

GARY: I went out with Big Pamela Davidson?

TOMMY: You know you did.

GARY: I was hopin' you'd forget about that little detail.

TOMMY: I remember everything about that night, especially the sounds of you giving her one in your sleeping bag.

GARY: You heard that?

TOMMY: The whole of County Down heard it.

GARY: Alright, alright. No need to remind me. I've been tryin' to block it out for the past twenty odd years.

TOMMY: I didn't hear you complaining at the time.

GARY: Yeah well, a poke is a poke when yer at that age.

TOMMY: Lovely.

GARY: It was one a the best nights a my life that night. Everytime I come down here, I remember the crack we had - the fire we lit that almost suffocated us - Elaine's shitty moods - the smell a peach flavoured Concorde wine which she spilt all over Big Pamela's bloody sleepin' bag. It was a great night.

TOMMY: You know what I remember? I remember you and me skinny dipping and me having to stay in the water for ages waiting for my

181

dick to go down. I remember you lifting me up and kissing me on the forehead when I agreed that *I Know It's Over* was a far superior song to *There's A Light That Never Goes Out.* I remember the reflection of the fire in your pupils and thinking how fucking beautiful you were. And I remember how I wanted to stick my hand in that same hot fire to block out the pain of seeing you doing Big Pamela Davidson in that bloody sleeping bag. That's what I remember.

Silence.

GARY: It's going to be an aquarium, you know.

TOMMY: What?

GARY: They're knockin' it down to build an aquarium. Oh aye tourism's booming, haven't you heard?

TOMMY: There's nothing wrong with that, Gaz. At least things are moving in the right direction.

GARY: Havin' to spend a tenner just to see a couple a oul crabs an' a bag of dolis is not what I call movin' in the right direction.

TOMMY: Better they're building things than blowing them up.

GARY: Aye, I suppose yer right.

Pause.

TOMMY: Will you do me a favour?

GARY: Dave?

Tommy nods.

TOMMY: Can you get him more time? I'm gonna try
and get it sorted out.

GARY: I'm not sure I can. He's rattled a few cages.

TOMMY: Come on. You owe me one. And think about
Elaine. It's not fair she should suffer
because of what he's done.

GARY: Okay, I'll see what I can do. But Listen
Millsey, Elaine's not as innocent as you
think. She knew what Dave was up to.

TOMMY: I don't think so.

GARY: She must have done. The wages from
Dave's wee paintin' and decoratin' job
hardly pays enough to open a sex shop.
Think about it, Tommy. The money for the
sex shop had to come from somewhere else.
Yer not tryin' to tell me she thought he'd
won the lottery or somethin'?

Scene 9

The following evening. The Dining-room. Elaine sits at the table, smoking. Tommy enters from the back door.

ELAINE: Tommy, thank God. I've been up the high doe worrying about you.

TOMMY: Where's Dave?

ELAINE: He plays pool on Tuesday.

TOMMY: When's he back?

ELAINE: About eleven, usually.

TOMMY: Right.

ELAINE: What's the matter?

TOMMY: I just want to get this mess sorted out once and for all, so I can get as far away from here as possible.

ELAINE: What's goin' on?

TOMMY: Just tell me one thing - and I want a straight answer - where did the money for the shop come from?

Pause.

ELAINE: The drugs.

TOMMY: And you knew that?

Silence.

For fuck sake!

ELAINE: Just hear me out, Tommy. The first I knew
             about the money was when Dave threw the
             lease papers at me. Up until that point I
             knew nothin' about his dealin'. Nothin' - I
             swear it. When he told me where he got the
             money from I hit the roof. I told him I
             didn't want anything to do with it. But he
             said he wanted to open the shop as a way
             out a the dealin'. He promised me it would
             be a new start for both of us. What was I to
             do? I had to give it a chance - give him a
             chance. If the shop worked and he didn't
             have to deal anymore, then it was worth
             givin' it a go. What choice did I have?

TOMMY: You could have left him.

ELAINE: Not everyone takes the easy way out,
             Tommy.

TOMMY: What's that supposed to mean?

Dave enters from the back door.

DAVE: You here again. If I didn't know you were
             queer, I'd think you were after my missus.
             (*To Elaine*) You'd like that, wouldn't you
             dear?

186

ELAINE: Don't talk shite.

DAVE: She always did prefer you to me.

ELAINE: Take no notice, Tommy.

DAVE: You know even on our weddin' day, when the photographer asked the happy couple to cut the cake, I half-expected her to grab you.

ELAINE: Fuck off, Dave.

TOMMY: (*To Dave*) You can have the money. I'm going to re-mortgage the house.

Pause.

ELAINE: No, Tommy. We don't want yer money.

DAVE: Shut it you.

TOMMY: I've made up my mind, Elaine.

DAVE: Do you mean it?

TOMMY: Yes Dave, I fuckin' mean it. But only if you give fifteen grand to the Boys and stop the dealing.

ELAINE: You don't have to do this, Tommy.

TOMMY: If it stops all this madness then it's worth it. It's up to you now.

Pause.

DAVE: Looks like it's an offer I can't refuse.

TOMMY: Right. I can get my hands on the fifteen by Thursday. You'll have to wait for the re-mortgage to come through before you get the rest. Is that okay?

Dave nods.

                   I'll take it to The Boys on Thursday night.

DAVE: I can do my own dirty work.

TOMMY: No, I'll do it.

DAVE: Don't you trust me?

TOMMY: No, I don't.

DAVE: Please yerself.

Tommy goes to leave.

                   Tommy?

He turns round. Dave struggles to say something. Tommy exits.

ELAINE: If I catch you givin' as much as a paracetamol to anyone ever again, I'll kill you myself. And I mean that, Dave.

DAVE: I promise babes. Now why don't we go upstairs and have another go at landing ourselves a wee Mister or Miss Mills? What do you say?

188

ELAINE: Fuck away off.

She exits.

Scene 10

The Air-Raid Shelter. Tommy hands Gary an envelope full of bank notes. Gary looks in it.

GARY: Did Dave give you it?

TOMMY: Does it matter?

GARY: He's got a very special brother.

TOMMY: Or a very stupid one.

GARY: You've saved his life.

TOMMY: Will that be the end of it then?

GARY: As long as he's not caught dealin' again.

TOMMY: Right.

Gary puts the envelope into his jacket pocket.

GARY: You know none a this is for me. I'm just the messenger.

TOMMY: That doesn't make it any better, Gaz.

GARY: Ach don't be like that. Sit down with me for a bit.

TOMMY: I've done what I came to do.

He goes to leave.

GARY: Gone off me already, have you?

TOMMY:	The other night shouldn't have happened. And it's not gonna happen again.
GARY:	That's a shame. It was the best shag I've ever had.
TOMMY:	Fuck off, Gaz.
GARY:	It was.
TOMMY:	You're a liar.
GARY:	You've had better then?
TOMMY:	I'm not getting sucked into this.

Tommy goes to walk off again.

GARY:	Thought as much.

Tommy stops. He can't help himself.

TOMMY:	As a matter of fact, I've had much better.
GARY:	Who with?
TOMMY:	With my partner.
GARY:	Oh, yer *partner*.
TOMMY:	Yeah, my partner.
GARY:	So what's this partner called?
TOMMY:	Toby.
GARY:	Toby?

TOMMY: Yeah, Toby.

GARY: And why isn't Toby over here with you?

TOMMY: Because…

Pause.

GARY: Well?

TOMMY: It's none of your fucking business.

Gary laughs.

Piss off!

GARY: So this Toby one's a better lay than me?

TOMMY: There's no comparison.

GARY: Does he like The Smiths?

TOMMY: What's that got to do with anything?

GARY: Does he like The Smiths?

TOMMY: No. He hates them. He can't stand Morrissey's whining voice.

GARY: Ah.

TOMMY: It doesn't bother me. I stopped listenin' to The Smiths a long time ago.

GARY: And what about Morrissey's new stuff?

TOMMY: Not interested.

GARY:	So you've never listened to *You Are The Quarry*?
TOMMY:	Never.
GARY:	So if I asked you what you thought the best track on the album was, you wouldn't be able to tell me?
TOMMY:	Wouldn't have a clue.
GARY:	That's a pity coz if I had to take a guess, I'd say *Back to Camden* was yer favourite.

Tommy gradually smiles.

TOMMY:	Bastard! You think you're so smart.
GARY:	It's the best thing he's done since The Smiths split up.

Gary sings the chorus to Back to Camden by Morrissey.

TOMMY:	He's still got it.
GARY:	Would you shag him?
TOMMY:	Definitely. You?
GARY:	Too oul for me. I like 'em young.
TOMMY:	Is your wife young?
GARY:	Let's not go there.
TOMMY:	How long have you been married?

GARY:	Do we have to?
TOMMY:	Come on. I wanna know.
GARY:	Thirteen long years.
TOMMY:	And when did you start all this?
GARY:	When my Da died – three years ago.
TOMMY:	And you'd never been with a man before that?
GARY:	Na. What a waste, aye?
TOMMY:	So for all these years you've been hiding it?
GARY:	Not really. I just didn't know.
TOMMY:	You miraculously woke up one morning and thought, hey I think I'll start shaggin' men, that'll be fun.
GARY:	Don't be a smart ass.
TOMMY:	Well, come on.
GARY:	Look, I always knew there was somethin', but I kinda just ignored it. Then when the oul fella dropped dead something clicked and I decided it was time to start findin' out what it was.
TOMMY:	It's a pity you didn't start twenty years ago. You could have saved me a lot of heartache.

GARY:	Surely it wasn't that bad? (*Tommy nods.*) Sorry.

Long Pause

Do you fancy runnin' away with me?

TOMMY:	Into the sunset?
GARY:	I was thinkin' a somewhere over the rainbow.

They laugh.

GARY:	Or you could just come back hame to live.
TOMMY:	Let's not get carried away, Gaz. You've got a wife and three weans and I'm certainly not ready to chuck away my life for someone who's connected to the paramilitaries.
GARY:	What if I was to get out?
TOMMY:	Would they let you?
GARY:	I could ask.

Pause.

TOMMY:	Look, I don't wanna talk about this. It's crazy. I've got a great guy back in Manchester, a job that I love... and a bloody fantastic allotment. I'd be fuckin' mad to throw it all away for a twat like you.

195

GARY:	Thanks a lot.
TOMMY:	Well you're hardly a catch.
GARY:	Alright, so yer not gonna spend the rest a yer life with me, but how about a few days campin' down here. We could pitch up a tent. It'id be great. I'll bring a few crates a beer, my Smiths CDs and a couple a hundred of condoms. What d'you say?
TOMMY:	I don't like beer.
GARY:	Come on. What else have you got to do? The Dave situation is sorted out.
TOMMY:	There's Toby.
GARY:	Tell him you an' Dave are gettin' reacquainted or somethin'. Come on, Millsey. We'll have a ball. What d'you say?
TOMMY:	I'm not sure.
GARY:	Come on. (*Pause.*) What would Morrissey do if he were in yer position?
TOMMY:	He'd walk away.
GARY:	It's a good job yer not him then. Now come on. Don't be a wee pansy all of yer life.

Tommy looks as if he's thinking about it. Lights down.

ACT TWO

Scene 1

The following week at the air-raid shelter. Afternoon. A tent has been erected in the bushes beside it. We hear water splashing and Tommy and Gary shouting off-stage.

GARY: Come back in, you wimp!

TOMMY: Fuck away off. It's freezin'.

Tommy appears wearing nothing but a towel. He's been skinny dipping. He goes into the tent and grabs a pair of shorts and a tee-shirt. He puts them on. His mobile phone rings. He picks it up and can't decide whether to answer it. He finally turns it off and then shouts to Gary in the Lough.

TOMMY: Get your big hairy arse up here and stop showing off!

Tommy proceeds to make a cup of tea using a small gas camping stove. Gary appears in a towel.

GARY: There's nothin' like an oul dip in the lough to get the blood pumpin'.

He lifts his towel.

TOMMY: Put Mighty Mouse away.

GARY: Where do you want me to put him?

TOMMY: Nowhere near me. I've had enough of that thing. It's been non-stop since we got here.

GARY: What do you expect? I'm practically a virgin.

TOMMY: You were never a virgin. You probably came out of the womb with an erection.

GARY: Funny you should say that.

TOMMY: Put it away for God's sake.

Gary laughs and starts to dress.

Do you want a cup of tea?

GARY: Na, I'll have a beer.

Gary grabs a beer and opens it.

Was that my phone ringin'?

TOMMY: No. It was Toby.

GARY: Did you speak to him?

TOMMY: I switched it off.

GARY: You should speak to him. He might be gettin' suspicious.

TOMMY: You may find it easy lying to people, but I don't.

GARY: So you'd rather he was worried sick not hearin' from you?

TOMMY: I'll speak to him when I'm ready – not when you tell me to. Okay?

GARY: Alright, alright. I was only sayin'.

TOMMY: And anyway, what about you? Aren't you worried that *her indoors* will be getting suspicious?

GARY: She's used to it. I'm always disappearin' for days on end when I'm doin' the business with The Boys.

TOMMY: Stop there. I don't want to hear about the bloody Boys.

GARY: I wasn't gonna say anything.

TOMMY: Good.

Pause.

GARY: Right. Here's one for you. *Heaven Knows I'm Miserable Now* or *Girlfriend In A Coma?*

TOMMY: Can't we talk about something other than Morrissey and the bloody Smiths for once?

GARY: Sorry if I'm borin' you. What would you like me to talk about? Quantum physics? The meltin' ice-caps? The Londonderry or Derry debate? I'm flexible me. I can talk about whatever you want.

TOMMY: Alright, let's talk about Derry then.

GARY: You mean, Londonderry.

TOMMY: Actually I mean Derry City after all that's the council's official name.

GARY: The city's official name is still Londonderry.

TOMMY: Does it matter?

GARY: Yeah, it does.

TOMMY: Why?

GARY: Because it's called Londonderry. That's why.

Tommy laughs.

TOMMY: I can't believe you actually care. What's happened to you, Mister McDaid?

GARY: Look, the Protestant people are makin' enough concessions as it is. We're bein' asked to change too quickly, that's all I'm sayin'.

TOMMY: At least you're being asked. When the British changed all the town names to English names at the turn of last century no-one bothered to ask the Irish if they minded.

GARY: Christ, if I'd known I was sleepin' with a Republican I would've brought my Tricolor tent with me.

TOMMY: You've become a right wee Proddie bastard.

GARY: And you've become a right wee smart cunt.

Gary jumps on him.

TOMMY: Get off, you orange bastard!

GARY: Taig lover!

They play fight finishing on their backs.

GARY: I tell you one thing. If global warmin' means weather like this, then I'm all for it.

TOMMY: Don't you think it's funny, Gaz, that the Province is getting its act together just as the rest of the world is falling to pieces? Look at Afghanistan and Iraq, Libya and the middle bloody east. It's all kicking off, yet we're having a relatively good time. It's mad.

GARY: It doesn't surprise me coz we're a contrary bunch. Take a roomful a people sayin' white and there in the middle a them you'll find an Ulsterman sayin' black. We like to be different. That's how we know we exist.

TOMMY: Do you think it will last – the peace?

GARY: Probably not.

TOMMY: Why not?

GARY: Too many people wantin' it to fail.

TOMMY: People like you?

GARY: I don't want it to fail.

TOMMY: Then why are you still playing cowboys and Indians with the Boys?

Gary is annoyed. Pause.

TOMMY: *Girlfriend In A Coma.*

GARY: What?

TOMMY: *Girlfriend In A Coma* is a far superior song to *Heaven Knows* because it perfectly illustrates what The Smiths were about. Wonderful melodies matched to dark, ironic lyrics. It's definitely the better song.

GARY: No way!

TOMMY: It is.

GARY: Look, I'll admit the contrast between the light, catchy chords and the ironic lyrics in *Girlfriend* make it irresistible, but the sheer brilliance of the lyrics in *Heaven Knows* make it the better song. End of argument.

TOMMY: Ach your taste is in your arse, so it is.

GARY: Na, my taste is in yer arse.

Gary kisses him.

TOMMY: Sorry about... I shouldn't have brought it up.

GARY: It's okay. Yer right. Things aren't gonna change here until bastards like me change.

TOMMY: And are you going to?

Pause.

GARY: Let's go for another swim. Come on. Last one in has to give the other a blow job.

Gary jumps up and runs towards the Lough. Tommy follows him.

TOMMY: Hey...!

Scene 2

The Sex shop. Elaine is putting sexy underwear onto hangers.
The phone rings.

ELAINE: Hello, Naughty but Nice. (*Pause*) Yes. (*Pause*) Oh, hi. (*Pause*) Ahm... he's not here. He's out with Dave some... where. (*Pause*) He might have left his phone at ours or... somethin'. (*Pause*) Everything's fine. He's just been... been busy catchin' up with everyone and gettin' to know Dave again. (*Pause*) Course I will. (*Pause*) I've heard a lot about you as well.

Dave enters and starts to pace up and down.

Definitely. (*Pause*) Thanks, Toby. I'll hold you to that. (*Pause*) Listen I have to go. Someone's just come into the shop. (*Pause*) Yes, look forward to it. (*Pause*) Bye.

Dave slams a packet of contraceptive pills onto the counter.

DAVE: What the fuck are those?

ELAINE: They're an old packet.

DAVE: Yer fuckin' lying!

Pause.

ELAINE: Dave, honey ...

DAVE: Lying fuckin' bitch!

204

ELAINE:	The timing's not right, Dave. The para's, the threats... I can't bring a baby into all this.
DAVE:	If it was Tommy's wean you wouldn't fuckin' mind.
ELAINE:	That's crap and you know it.
DAVE:	You've been playing me for a soft cunt. All these fuckin' years.
ELAINE:	Dave, hon...
DAVE:	Just admit it for fuck sake?
ELAINE:	Dave, we're too old now for weans.
DAVE:	Bollocks!
ELAINE:	I've never been the mothering type. It's got nothing to do with you. It's me.
DAVE:	Liar!
ELAINE:	We can be happy just the way we are. We don't need anything else.
DAVE:	I want a fuckin' wean!
ELAINE:	Dave... please. In yer heart, do you really think you'd... we'd make good parents? Be honest, Dave.
DAVE:	Yer taking no more of these fuckin' pills. Do you hear!

He grabs her. She stares him out until he lets go.

ELAINE: There's not going to be any weans, Dave.
I've made up my mind.

DAVE: Then we're finished.

He exits.

ELAINE: Dave!

Scene 3

Night. The air-raid shelter. A Smiths CD is playing on a portable CD player. Tommy and Gary are playing cards.

GARY: Jack change it to... hearts.

Tommy smiles and puts down two cards.

TOMMY: Miss a go. Miss another go. And pick up two.

GARY: You jammie bastard.

Gary picks up two cards.

TOMMY: Jack changes it to... spades. And last card.

GARY: You fucker.

Gary picks up a card and Tommy places his last one down on the pile.

TOMMY: Thank you very much. That's... oh my god, fifty pence you owe me.

GARY: Don't worry. You'll get every penny of it back, even if I have to break into the Northern Bank to get it. Now deal us in.

TOMMY: I've had enough.

GARY: Come on, give us a chance to win some of it back.

TOMMY: No. I just wanna lie here and look at the sky for a bit.

He lies down.

GARY: I'm gettin' a beer.

TOMMY: I can't believe how clear it is.

GARY: Aye, you can see Uranus.

Tommy gives him a disdainful look. Gary sits down next to him with his beer.

TOMMY: The moon looks different here than in England. Seriously, it looks different. (*Pause*) Maybe every country has its own moon. Have you ever thought of that?

GARY: Yer a space cadet, that's what I think.

TOMMY: You've no imagination that's your trouble. (*Pause.*) Are you a believer, Gaz?

GARY: A believer in what?

TOMMY: Fucking vampires, what do you think?

GARY: I believe in what I can see an' what I can touch.

TOMMY: So you don't think there's anything after life?

GARY: No.

TOMMY:　　Nothing?

GARY:　　Yeah, nothin'. A big Zilch.

TOMMY:　　God, you're so poetic.

GARY:　　Why? Do you believe?

TOMMY:　　Sometimes.

GARY:　　My oul fella used to say that each man is like the leadin' man in his own fillum an' when the leadin' man dies or gets killed, then that's it - the fillum ends. I kinda agree with him.

TOMMY:　　You loved your oul man, didn't you?

GARY:　　Aye.

TOMMY:　　What would he have thought if he'd known you were...

GARY:　　What? Involved with the Boys?

TOMMY:　　It doesn't matter.

GARY:　　He would have kicked my arse in.

Pause.

TOMMY:　　Gaz, I wanna ask you something. And I want a straight answer, okay?

GARY:　　I'm all ears.

TOMMY:　　Have you murdered people?

Pause.

GARY: Thought you didn't want to hear about all
              that.

TOMMY: I need to know.

GARY: Why?

TOMMY: I just do.

GARY: What difference will it make?

TOMMY: I don't know until I hear your answer.

Gary doesn't answer.

              Well?

GARY: I've done a few knee-caps...

TOMMY: Jesus!

GARY: ...but that's about it.

TOMMY: That's okay then!

GARY: Well you asked.

TOMMY: I didn't want details.

GARY: Well now you know. I'm a bad boy.

TOMMY: It's not fucking funny, Gaz. You actually
              hurt people. I don't know how you can go
              to bed and sleep at nights. I mean, how can
              you go home and face your own family

when you've just destroyed someone elses? What type of man can do that?

GARY: I'm good at blockin' things out.

TOMMY: Well, maybe it's time you started facing up to the truth.

Gary's mobile phone rings.

GARY: Jesus Christ!

Gary looks at who's calling. He seems worried.

I better get this. (*He answers the phone.*) What is it? (*He moves away from Tommy and whispers into the phone.*) Can't you an' Marty sort it out? (*Beat*) Look Bill, I'm personally involved here... they're friends a mine. (*Beat*) Can't he get someone else to do it? (*Beat*) For fuck sake. (*Beat*) Okay. Tell him I'll be there in the mornin'. (*Beat*) No, the mornin'. It can wait till then.

He throws the mobile down.

TOMMY: Well? Who was it?

GARY: I've got to go back in the mornin'.

TOMMY: What for?

GARY: ...Business.

TOMMY:	What kind of... oh no, Gaz. Whatever it is, don't do it. Please, don't do it.
GARY:	I'm not. I've had enough. I'm gonna tell them I want out.
TOMMY:	Do you mean it? You're not just saying that for my benefit?
GARY:	I'm fed up with it. I'm sick a bein' at their beck an' call all the time. I've had enough. You've made me see the light.
TOMMY:	You won't be in any danger, will you?
GARY:	Na, course not.
TOMMY:	Are you sure?
GARY:	I'm sure.
TOMMY:	I'll come with you.
GARY:	Don't talk shite. Anyhow I want you to stay here till I get back. We've still got a couple a days left.
TOMMY:	Gaz, I don't want you to put yourself in danger on my account. (*Pause*) I can't promise you anything.
GARY:	I'm doin' it for me, so don't worry. And anyway, nothin's gonna happen. I'm one a their own.

Scene 4

The Sex shop. The following morning. Elaine opens the shop and enters. She takes her mobile out and makes a call.

ELAINE: It's me again. I know yer listenin' to these messages luv, so please ring back. Look I'm worried sick. I couldn't sleep a wink last night thinking about where you where an' what you were doin'. Just let me know yer okay, that's all I want. And Dave, I don't know how many times you expect me to say this, but it's nothing to do with you. It's me. And that's the truth, so please luv ring me back when you get this message. Or come down to the shop for a wee talk. Just don't do anything stupid, Dave. Please. Please luv.

She hangs up and goes into the backroom to make a tea. The door opens and she runs out expecting Dave. It's two men wearing balaclavas and holding guns. One of them is Gary. He stays near the door as look-out.

MAN: Where's Dave?

ELAINE: He's not here.

MAN: Where the fuck is he?

ELAINE: I don't know.

He pushes her to the side and looks into the back room.

213

I told you, he's not here. Now what's this
about? You got yer money, didn't you?

He goes back to her and puts a gun to her head.

MAN: Yer fuckin' bastard of a husband has been
                dealin' again. Now where is he? Tell me!

ELAINE: I don't know.

MAN: Tell me!

GARY: She said she doesn't know. Now leave her.

Elaine realises it's Gary.

ELAINE: Does yer boyfriend know what yer up to,
                Gary?

MAN: Shut yer mouth! What's she talkin' about?

GARY: I don't know. Now come on.

MAN: Where's yer mobile?

ELAINE: It's here.

MAN: Ring him.

ELAINE: There's no point. He's not answerin' it.

MAN: Ring him!

ELAINE: Okay, okay.

She calls him.

MAN: Give it here.

She hands him the phone. He puts it to his ear. It goes to the answer phone.

           Bastard! (*Beat*) Has it got a video camera?

GARY: What the fuck are you doin'?

MAN: Has it?

ELAINE: Yes.

MAN: Turn it on. Quick!

Elaine puts the phone to camera.

           Now give it here.

GARY: Fuck sake! Stop fuckin' around.

MAN: Shut it you.

He holds the phone up towards Elaine and presses record. He then fires the gun. Elaine screams and ducks to the floor. The bullet smashes into the head of a mannequin behind Elaine.

MAN: Get up. Get up! (*She gets up.*) Now send it to him. Come on!

She takes the phone and does it.

           Tell that drug-dealin' fuckin' piece a shit a yers that we're lukin for him, and if we don't find him we'll be back lukin for you

215

instead. And by the way - as of now, yer knockin' off shop is closed.

Gary and the other para run out. Elaine immediately grabs her mobile and rings Dave.

ELAINE: Dave, listen to me. Yer gonna have to get out a the country. Don't go back to the house whatever you do. Just get out a the country. I'll be alright. Go to Tommy's in Manchester. I'll find him an' make sure it's alright. Don't worry about me. I can look after myself. Now call me back when you get this message and please luv, don't try to be the big man.

She hangs up and rings Tommy.

Come on Tommy, answer the bloody phone.

She throws the phone into her handbag and exits.

Scene 5

The air-raid shelter. Tommy is on the phone to Toby.

TOMMY: I've been busy. Dave and I have been out a lot. (*Pause*) The battery was dead. (*Pause*) It's the truth. (*Pause*) No, nothing's the matter. (*Pause*) Alright, alright something has happened. (*Pause*) I'm not talking about it now. (*Pause*) No, wait till I get back. (*Pause*) Please babe... don't make this difficult for me. (*Pause*) We'll talk about it then. (*Pause*) No. (*Pause*) No, I'm not... Don't be silly. We just need to talk. I'll be back in a few days.

We hear a car pull up. Tommy stands up to see who it is.

Look, I'm going to have to go. I'll ring you tonight. (*Pause*) Yes, I promise. (*Pause*) Okay.

Elaine enters. He hangs up.

What's the matter? You look like shit.

ELAINE: Where's yer boyfriend, Tommy?

TOMMY: He's had to go back.

ELAINE: You don't say.

TOMMY: What's going on?

ELAINE: Do you want me to tell you what he's been
            up to this mornin'? Or would you rather
            bury yer head in the fuckin' sand?

TOMMY: Just tell me, Elaine.

ELAINE: Yer precious Gary McDaid has been puttin'
            bullets into my shop walls. (*Pause.*) That's
            right, Tommy. And if he finds Dave he'll be
            puttin' bullets into him as well.

TOMMY: Are you sure it was Gary?

ELAINE: Of course I'm sure.

TOMMY: Did you see his face?

ELAINE: It was him!

Pause.

TOMMY: He told me he was getting out.

ELAINE: And you believed him?

TOMMY: He meant it.

ELAINE: Wake up, Tommy. He said the exact same
            thing to me fifteen years ago. What makes
            you think it'll be any different for you?

Tommy is shocked.

            Yes that's right – me and Gary McDaid.

TOMMY: But you never liked him.

218

ELAINE: It just happened. One night down at The Oul Cross we got pissed and started talkin' about you and the good oul days. Six months later I was still with him, still pissed, but goin' nowhere fast. Then Dave found me, sobered me up and straightened me out. End a story. Now come on. We have to find Dave an' get him out of the country. He'll have to go to yers? (*Tommy is unsure.*) He's yer brother, for fuck sake.

TOMMY: I've got Toby to think about.

ELAINE: You weren't thinkin' about Toby when you were down here fuckin' the ass off Gary McDaid. Now come on Tommy, he's got nowhere else to go.

Scene 6

Later. Kitchen/diner. Dave sits in the dark, waiting. On the table in front of him sits his mobile, an opened bag of coke and a debit card. Elaine and Tommy enter from the kitchen door.

ELAINE: I'll try his mobile again.

She turns the lights on.

                 Dave! (*She runs over to him.*) Come on, luv. We've to get you outta here. Yer gonna go to Tommy's.

DAVE: I'm goin' nowhere.

ELAINE: Dave...

DAVE: Why don't you have a few lines with me? Come on.

TOMMY: There's no time for fuckin' around, Dave.

ELAINE: They'll kill you.

DAVE: Not before I take a few a them with me.

He pulls out a pistol from his jacket pocket.

ELAINE: Jesus, no.

TOMMY: Great! Fuckin' great.

DAVE: What's the matter, Tommy? Worried I'll put a bullet through yer boyfriend's head?

ELAINE: There's no time for this.

TOMMY: What's the point, Elaine? Look at him. He's a loser. Couldn't keep off the drugs for one week.

ELAINE: Tommy, stop…

TOMMY: He doesn't care about / you…

ELAINE: Shut up, Tommy. It's my fault he's gone back to the drugs, so just leave it.

TOMMY: No Elaine, I won't leave it. He doesn't care about anyone but himself. He never has done. So let him sit here and get killed if he wants to. He's gonna end up dead anyway.

DAVE: Now yer talkin'. That's a boy. Get it all out. Stick yer fingers down yer throat an' bring it all up.

ELAINE: Stop it you two! Just stop it.

Pause.

DAVE: Did you know that when the oul doll was up those stairs rottin' away with cancer she never once thanked me for bein' there – for houlin' her hand. Not once did she say, thank you son. (*Pause*) It was all about you Tommy. Where's Tommy? When's the wean comin' over? Even when she was off her face on morphine thinkin' she was thirty-six again, it was all about how good

221

the wean was – how beautiful he looked in his Bay City Rollers outfit. It was like I'd never existed. I even pretended to be you one night. Can you believe that? Just to give her one night a peace. I sat there beside her talkin' a load of shite about things I knew nothin' about. Laughing with her and noddin' my head like fuckin' Noddy as I pretended to remember things you and her used to do together. How do you think that made me feel, Tommy? Knowing that my own Ma didn't give a shit about me – that she only cared for her wee son – that same wee son who refused to come over an' see her just because of some silly fuckin' argument they'd had.

TOMMY: She said all queers should be shot.

DAVE: Fuck sake, you know what she was like. She was always spoutin' off - sayin' things she didn't mean.

TOMMY: I know. But I just wanted her to know that she'd really hurt me this time.

DAVE: Don't worry, she got yer message loud and clear.

ELAINE: Dave, luv. We should go. You and Tommy can talk about this later when yer at his.

TOMMY: Look, I made a mistake. I know that. I've said I'm sorry. I can't do any more Dave.

Pause.

DAVE: I never hated you. Do you know that? (*Beat*) I always stood up for you. When you weren't looking of course. Couldn't have you knowin' about it. But I was always there. Whenever anyone took the piss and called you a queer bastard, I sorted them out - afterwards. Did you know that?

TOMMY: Yes. Yes, I did.

DAVE: Of course you did.

Pause.

ELAINE: Dave luv, if you promise to come to Tommy's I'll think about the wean. Now come...

Suddenly the kitchen door is kicked in and Gary, wearing a balaclava, bursts in. He sees Tommy and is unsure what to do. Dave pushes Elaine to the floor and goes to grab the gun. Gary shoots him and runs out. Elaine goes to Dave.

ELAINE: Dave... Dave... oh God. No... no, no, no...

Tommy picks Dave's gun up off the floor. Lights.

Scene 7

The air-raid shelter, night. The tent is still up. Gary sits beside it, head in hands. Tommy arrives. Gary stands up when he sees him. Tommy takes the gun out and points it at Gary.

GARY: Go on, Tommy. Do it. Just do it. I deserve it. I fuckin' deserve it.

TOMMY: Shut up! Shut the fuck up!

GARY: I had to do it, Tommy. You know that, don't you?

TOMMY: You said you were quitting. You said you were getting out.

GARY: One last job they said. One last job, Tommy. Or else the bullet was goin' into my head. That was the deal.

TOMMY: You should have taken the bullet. You should have stood there and said, 'go ahead lads go ahead, do what you have to do because I'm scum – I'm a piece of shit – I don't deserve to live – I'm a waste of fuckin' space!'

GARY: I know, I know.

TOMMY: He's my brother!

GARY: I know.

TOMMY:	How did you think I was going to take it? Slap you on the wrist, then drop to my knees and suck your knob and forget it ever happened?
GARY:	I thought... I thought... that in time... / maybe...
TOMMY:	Are you stupid? Are you fuckin' stupid? It's not going to happen.
GARY:	I'm free now, Tommy. It's over.
TOMMY:	Shut up!
GARY:	I can start again... we can / start...
TOMMY:	You're a dead man, Gaz. A dead fuckin' man!
GARY:	I don't have to be.
TOMMY:	Shut it!

He points the gun to Gary's head.

You know, stupidly enough for one second there I was beginning to believe there was a glimmer of hope for this place. I really believed it. Look at all the changes, I thought. Things are moving on. Good old *Norn Iron's* becoming the kind a place I'd like to come back to – to settle down in. I mean, look at Belfast. It's great. You can

225

now go shopping without fear of getting your limbs blown off. And look at Stormont with Paisley and McGuinness, the fuckin' chuckle brothers, standing side by side under the same roof as each other, pissing into the same fuckin' urinal. When did you ever think that would happen? And then there was you – about to give it all up for me. What a fuckin' joke! Nothing has changed, has it? Scratch the surface and the same stinkin' smell fills your nostrils and gangsters like you are still running the country.

GARY: Tommy listen to me. Yer right. This country stinks. It corrupts you and eats away at you. Just look at me. You *know* I wasn't like this to begin with – that I didn't give two shits about fenians and prods or what flag flew above my head. All that mattered to me was *'a light that never goes out'* and *'a boy with a thorn in his side.'* But this country changed me, Tommy. I don't know how or when, but it did. It's no excuse, I know, for what I've done, but it's over now. I can get out. Leave it all behind. Start again. And you can help me, Tommy.

TOMMY: And why would I do that, Gaz? Why would I help a murdering yellow bellied bastard like you?

GARY: Because... there's somethin' there... between us. A connection. I connect to you Tommy like I've never connected to anyone else before. And I know it's the same for you. You can't deny it. It's been there from the beginning. (*Pause*) Even on that night Tommy, when I was humpin' big Pamela Davidson in the sleepin' bag, I was imaginin' it was you. I swear it. My eyes were closed and all I could see was you. Even then. It's the God's honest truth. It's always been you.

Tommy charges at Gary and knocks him to the ground. They fight. Gary gets on top of him and holds him down. He tries to kiss him. Tommy manages to haul him off. He grabs the gun and points it at Gary who cowers on the ground.

TOMMY: Liar! Fuckin' liar! You fuckin' liar!

He wants to shoot him, but can't do it. Eventually he drops the gun and walks away. Gary gets up and takes hold of the gun.

GARY: Tommy don't walk away! Tommy! Come on, Tommy!

Desperately he starts to sing the chorus from 'There Is A Light That Never Goes Out'.

Tommy! To die by yer side... Tommy!

Tommy continues walking.

Tommy!

Gary points the gun at his back as he walks off. The lights snap out and we hear a shot.

The End.